Wales 1976

Back row (l. to r.): John Bevan, Mike Knill, Graham Price, Trevor Evans, Allan Martin, Geoff Wheel,
Charlie Faulkner, Bobby Windsor, Tom David, Steve Fenwick, Roy Bergiers, Derek Quinnell, Roy Thomas.
Front row: Brynmor Williams, Gerald Davies, J.P.R. Williams, Gareth Edwards, Mervyn Davies, Phil Bennett, J.J. Williams, Ray

Wales 1978
(L. to r.): Phil Bennett, Gareth Edwards, Ray Gravell, Steve Fenwick, Bobby Windsor,
Graham Price, Jeff Squire, Charlie Faulkner, Terry Cobner, J.J. Williams, Gareth Evans,
Geoff Wheel, Allan Martin, Derek Quinnell, J.P.R. Williams.

Welsh Rugby
in the
1970s

Originally published in
2015 by Gomer

Reprinted by Y Lolfa in
2023

ISBN 978 1 80099 398 3

A CIP record for this title is
available from the British
Library

This book was originally
published with the financial
support of the
Welsh Books Council.

The publishers would also
like to acknowledge the
generous contributions
made by Colorsport to the
publication of this book.

Printed in India by Imprint
Press

www.ylolfa.com
ylolfa@ylolfa.com

A monument in mud: Gareth Edwards's
immortal try against Scotland in 1972 is
celebrated in Elin Siân Blake's painting.
(Courtesy of the artist)

Welsh Rugby
in the
1970s

CAROLYN HITT

CONTENTS

INTRODUCTION
'We Are a Family'

(PA Images)

Cadbury's
curlywurly
CARAMEL COVERED
IN MILK CHOCOLATE
3P

CYMRU

DISCO

Like the trajectory of a Space Hopper, the 1970s was a decade that bounced in unexpected directions. From pop culture to politics, paradoxes abounded.

We sweated in cheesecloth through heatwave seasons in the sun… and shivered through uncollected bin bags in the Winter of Discontent. There were dark, drab times of strikes, power cuts and three-day weeks. But they were also lit up by the outrageous colour palette of our clothes and homes: purple flares, orange shagpile and avocado bathrooms.

Through the economic instability of four prime ministers, four general elections and five official states of emergency we still found laughter in a golden age of sitcom and grooved to a soundtrack that throbbed from glam rock to punk rock via a disco inferno.

Children cherished the lovable groan of Bagpuss, the incomprehensible lingo of The Clangers and the chewy delights of a Curly Wurly. And even though those terrifying 'Charley Says' public information films warned us of potentially fatal perils around every corner we went out to play with a freedom future generations could never enjoy.

In Wales another paradox was at play. It was the best of times. It was the worst of times. Built on the iconic toil of heavy industry, our sense of self was crumbling with every closing pit and steelworks. But another signifier of Cymric identity – first formed in the early years of the 20th century with a team that conquered the world – was thriving once more.

Rugby defined Wales in the 70s. As so many certainties of life in the industrialised valley communities were unravelling, success on the field of play remained as a constant and reassuring thread, tethering us to the romantic traditions of the past.

But as the achievement grew into unparalleled success – six Triple Crowns and three Grand Slams accomplished in dazzling style – it was clear Welsh rugby was creating a phenomenon that was rooted firmly in the present and unique to that decade.

New gods with pop-star hair and industrial-sized sideburns bestrode the turf of the Arms Park. The Outside Half Factory sent not one but two world-class fly-halves off the production line as Barry John was succeeded by Phil Bennett.

And in Gareth Edwards, both were partnered by a scrum-half who would be hailed the greatest player of all time. In the midfield the 70s centres ranged from John Dawes, the deftest of link men, to the direct and hard-running Steve Fenwick to the formidable *hwyl* of Ray Gravell who channelled the spirit of Owain Glyndŵr on every crash-ball surge.

On the right wing, the fleet-footed elegance of Gerald Davies turned rugby into an art form while J.J. Williams chipped and chased on the left with the pace of a Commonwealth sprinter. Then there was the running full-back JPR, thundering, socks down, into attack with almost manic determination.

And all this spectacular back play was made possible by the supply of great ball served up by a formidable Welsh pack. Was a front row ever more feted than the Pontypool trio of Graham Price, Bobby Windsor, and Charlie Faulkner? Unpick the locks of the 70s and you found players of the calibre of Delme Thomas, Geoff Wheel, Derek Quinnell and Allan Martin – a second row with the goal-kicking boot of an outside half.

At flanker Dai 'The Shadow' Morris threw his team-mates into the light, while John Taylor's soft hands, left foot and hard tackling added to the armoury of the back row.

Merve, meanwhile, never actually swerved but provided rock-steady captaincy and athletic dynamism at no.8.

The serendipity of so much talent combining made the 70s special. Yet while it is tempting to reflect on this golden rugby age as if it was an era conjured randomly out of Welsh mythology, the sorcery was underpinned by structural and social changes in Welsh sport.

The 70s generation benefited from an increased emphasis on specialist physical education teaching, as Gareth Edwards said: 'We were regarded as the last of the grammar/secondary modern school era. We were greatly influenced by a number of teachers who gave of their time lovingly. These PE masters were the first generation who had taken specialist PE degrees through places like St Lukes, Loughborough and Cardiff Training College and became out and out physical education teachers.'

So a talented but slight young athlete like Gerald Davies was introduced as a teenager to the concept of strength and conditioning: 'The PE master was influential in that he was saying, "Listen this is the game but you're not very big. If you want to pursue this game you need to toughen up a bit". So he was the one, who in a very rudimentary way, introduced me to weight training.'

Changes in the laws of the game allowed Welsh flair free rein. The 'Australian Dispensation' stopped a player from clearing directly to touch outside his own 22 (or 25, as it was then). Not only did this prevent the debacle of a mind-numbing match dominated by lineouts – 111 in the

The legendary Pontypool front row,
Price, Windsor and Faulkner.

infamous Scotland v Wales clash of 1963 – it encouraged creative attack and transformed the role of the full-back in particular.

And by the time the 70s generation were embarking on their international careers a structural revolution had taken place in the administration of Welsh rugby. In 1967 the shrewd and eloquent North Walian Ray Williams had been appointed the National Coaching Organiser for Wales – the first appointment of its kind in the world game.

From mini-rugby to the elite, this rugby visionary pioneered a system that by the mid-70s had produced 300 coaches and allowed such inspirational national coaches as Clive Rowlands to flourish.

According to Gerald Davies 'Clive had done everything in the game. He had captained Wales throughout his career. He had a very strong vision of Welsh rugby and what Welsh rugby meant to him. And in that period he transmitted to us as

Dai Morris in the thick of it, giving Mervyn Davies a piggy-back.

'Top Cat' Clive Rowlands, the indisputable leader of the gang.

Ray Williams

players how important rugby was for Wales. How important the jersey was. He gave a passionate sense of the value of rugby in Wales. And he gave us that sense of identity.'

There was also continuity. This was an international side with the camaraderie of a club, as Gareth Edwards recalled: 'The nucleus of that side lasted for a decade as 19-year-olds grew into mature players. And indeed one of the favourite sentiments of the selectors was "Boys, we are a family".'

'Boys, we are a family'

GARETH EDWARDS

T. G. R. DAVIES (Cambridge University)

Wing or centre. Born 7.2.45. 5 ft. 9 in., 11 st. 8 lb. Thomas Gerald Reames Davies was educated at Queen Elizabeth Grammar School, Carmarthen and Loughborough Colleges and is now in his third year of reading English at Cambridge. He first burst upon the first class scene in 1966.

when he helped Loughborough Colleges to win the Middlesex sevens by a record margin. He toured South Africa with Cardiff in 1967 and in that year he was given the first of his 15 Welsh caps. He toured South Africa with the British Lions in 1968 as a centre and he toured New Zealand, Australia and Fiji with Wales in 1969. He won Blues in 1968, 1969 and 1970 when he was captain of the defeated Cambridge team. Unavailable for international football last season, he regained his place in the Welsh team this season as a wing after making a great impression in that position in

T. G. R. DAVIES

Building Blocks (1969-71)

①

In 1969 Wales's home games were played in a building site as the National Stadium underwent a major redevelopment. The restricted crowds of 29,000 who took their place in the half-finished stands could see something else was being constructed on the field – a team that would dominate European rugby for the next 10 years.

In its transition phase, Wales took the Triple Crown and Championship that season – off the back of the first ever national squad training sessions at the Afan Lido. Success in '69 may have been built on the sands of Aberavon but the firmest of foundations had been laid.

In October 1970 the refurbished stadium was unveiled in all its concrete-ramparted glory, an impressive new north stand offering seated comfort for the faithful. The stage was set for a decade of compelling drama.

J. C. BEVAN
J. C. BEVAN (Cardiff College of Education)
Wing. Born 28.10.50 at Llwynnypia in the Rhondda.
6 ft., 13 st.

1971 – The first Grand Slam

With no more than 16 men in action through the season a team of joie de vivre and enterprise captured a prize that had eluded Welsh rugby since 1952. The glamour club of London Welsh contributed six players – including captain John Dawes – and their influence could be seen in the attractive attacking brand of rugby Wales delivered.

Gerald Davies – back from his academic sabbatical from international rugby at Cambridge – confirmed Clive Rowlands' decision to switch him from centre to wing was a masterstroke. On the opposite wing, strapping Rhondda athlete John Bevan complemented TGR's panache with raw power.

The wings provided all the tries in Wales's thrilling demolition of England in the opening game of the championship. Twenty-year-old Bevan scored on his debut, while Gerald crossed twice in the corner. Left-footed conversions by John Taylor sent Wales 16–3 ahead at half-time. A penalty from JPR – who stayed on the field despite a broken cheekbone – two dropped goals from Barry John, and vigorous scrummaging from the Welsh pack ensured England barely got a look in. Final score: 22–6.

But the key game of the 1971 campaign was against Scotland where Wales snatched victory two minutes from the final whistle in a pulsating Celtic clash that saw the lead change hands six times. One final attack from a stolen Scottish lineout created a stylish three-quarter move spreading from left to right to send Gerald Davies curving across the line. But a Welsh win depended on a tricky conversion.

J. TAYLOR

J. TAYLOR (London Welsh)
Flanker. Born 21.7.45. 5 ft. 11 in., 13 st. 7 lb. John Taylor was educated at Watford Grammar School and Loughborough Colleges and played only four first-class games as a flanker before winning a place in the Welsh final trial in 1967. He began his international career against Scotland in the same year and the following year was chosen to tour South Africa with the British Lions. He lost his place in the Welsh team because of his political objections to playing against South Africa but was recalled to the team at the end of last season. With his left-footed, round the corner style, he kicked two very important conversions in the mud and rain against England but then surpassed himself against Scotland. He scored a remarkable try and then, with the fate of the whole match depending on the success of his difficult kick at goal after Gerald Davies' try, he drilled the ball straight through the middle and won the match by one point. The Welsh Rugby Union plan to put the left boot which did it in a glass exhibition case! Taylor is a schoolmaster and has won 16 caps.

John Dawes gave the kick from the right-hand touchline to left-footed flanker John Taylor. With his beard and halo of frizz, Taylor may have looked like a 70s wild man of rock but there was nothing wayward about the precision he brought to his kicking. As a nation peeped through its fingers, he stepped up coolly and slotted the ball over the posts to seal a memorable triumph.

Back on home soil the Triple Crown was secured with an emphatic 23–9 defeat of Ireland, as Gareth Edwards and Gerald Davies divided four tries between them while Barry John's boot brought two penalties, a conversion and a drop goal.

A delirious crowd descended from the stands and chaired several players off the pitch to a chant of 'We are the champions'. An extra celebration arrived for 13 of the side on the field that day as, ahead of their final game, they learned they had been selected for the 1971 Lions tour to New Zealand.

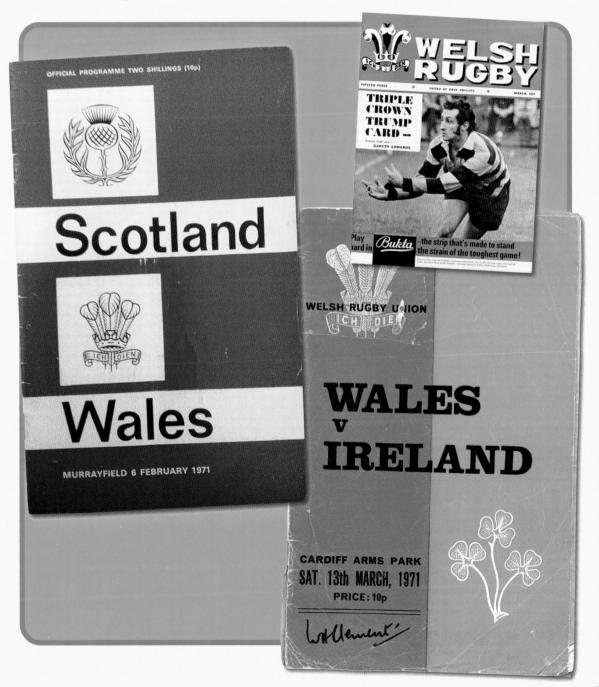

The Grand Slam was in sight but it required a challenging trip to France where Wales had not won for 14 years. Unbeaten that season, Les Bleus were aiming for a share of the championship – although their drawn games against England and Ireland meant only Wales could win the Grand Slam outright.

Against the backdrop of Stade Colombes – where Wales were playing for the final time – an enthralling encounter unfolded. In the first half, JPR created a stunning try for Gareth Edwards after stealing Roger Bourgarel's pass deep in the Welsh half and racing 70 yards to deliver the scoring pass.

In the second half, Barry John – nursing a broken nose from his heroic tackle on big Benoit Dauga – popped a straightforward penalty over and scored a trademark weaving try. A record crowd of 60,000 witnessed the Welsh Grand Slam that ignited the golden era.

Ray Williams told the 1971 AGM of the WRU that 'Welsh rugby has been transformed… radically changed.' And there was plenty more magic to come.

france-galles
TOURNOI DES CINQ NATIONS
COLOMBES 27 MARS 1971 _ PROGRAMME OFFICIEL _ PRIX 1,50 F (FFR)

B. DAUGA

B. DAUGA (Mont-de-Marsan)
No. 8 or lock. Born 8.5.42 at Mont Gaillard. 6 ft. 5 in. 15 st. 7 lb. Benoit Dauga is probably the greatest forward France has ever produced and since he first played for his country in 1964, he has won 49 caps and has earned the respect of the best forwards in the world. He thus wins his

B. JOHN (Cardiff)
Outside-half. Born 6.1.45. 5 ft. 9 in., 11 st. 11 lb. Barry John was educated at Gwendraeth Grammar School and at Trinity College, Carmarthen. He began his first class career with Llanelli. First capped against Australia in 1966, he was chosen for the British Lions tour of South Africa in 1968, by which time he had joined Cardiff. His collar bone was broken early on and he only played four games on tour. Played against New Zealand twice and against Australia on the Welsh tour of New Zealand, Australia and Fiji in 1968. He played one of the greatest games of his career against England this season when he dropped two goals and made a try. Against Scotland he scored an astonishing try and kicked a penalty goal and made a conversion. When he is stimulated sufficiently by the occasion, he seems capable almost of anything. He works in a finance house and has won 20 caps.

Also in 1971: This year brought two significant milestones for the Welsh language as the Welsh Nursery Movement was founded and it became legal to register marriages in Welsh. Homegrown showbiz talent was making an impact on British television as Ryan and Ronnie transferred their successful Welsh-language show to BBC1, while Nerys Hughes got her big break in *The Liver Birds*. Mary Hopkin got hitched to record producer Tony Visconti, and John Dawes was awarded Welsh Sports Personality of the Year.

Ryan and Ronnie (BBC)

The Liver Birds

WRU CENTENARY 1881-1981

John Dawes

'Which way do I go now?' Gareth Edwards is blocked by the combined headbands of Denzil Williams (left), Mervyn Davies and Mike Roberts.

Player Profile
BARRY JOHN

If the 70s was the era of Glam Rock, Barry John was the embodiment of Glam Rugby. He was the first true celebrity not only of the Welsh game but the world game. It was, after all, the rugby public of New Zealand who crowned the fly-half 'The King' after they thrilled to his fabulous performance on the 1971 Lions tour.

He had it all – pin-up good looks; charisma and wit and a unique playing style of gliding, ghosting beauty and pinpoint kicking.

Yet just like many rock stars of the era, Barry left the stage too soon – hanging up his boots suddenly at the age of just 27.

An oval ball brain: As a sixth former at Gwendraeth Grammar School, he lay awake at night dreaming up new moves to try on the rugby field, penning them in his bedside notebook. By the time he was at his peak, he did not have to resort to writing them down. Barry surveyed the scene like a general plotting his battle campaign, always several moves ahead of the opposition.

The early years: Cefneithin, Carwyn and Coventry City: Barry shared his home village of Cefneithin with Carwyn James, the Llanelli fly-half who would coach the Lions to glory against the All Blacks. The young boy's hero would become the young player's mentor… and allow him to play football during rugby training sessions. Barry's round ball skills almost lured him to Coventry City as a youth.

The rugby family tree: His brother Del captained the village team, while both siblings Alan and Clive John played for Llanelli. His sister Madora, meanwhile, married Derek Quinnell, ensuring the John genes were passed to another fine generation of Welsh rugby talent – Scott, Craig and Gavin.

(Getty Images)

THE STATS Wales: **25** Caps British & Irish Lions: **5** Caps

The perfect partnership: Edwards and John…it was a half-back combo made in heaven. When Barry met Gareth they bonded with a typically nonchalant quip from the fly-half. The latter was anxious for a practice session ahead of winning his first Welsh cap. Meeting up on the field of Trinity College, Carmarthen with a bleary-eyed, dap-wearing Barry – he'd been partying the night before and couldn't find his boots – Gareth was desperate to discuss ball service tactics. But Barry had a simpler solution: 'You just throw it and I'll catch it,' he said.

The glory years: Barry was already showing glimpses of his prodigious talent with the Lions in South Africa in 1968 but a broken collarbone in the first Test cut short his tour. In 1969 he helped Wales to the championship in the season that proved the springboard for the golden generation of the following decade. A mesmerising try against England confirmed Barry's special qualities to an entranced public. But it was 1971 that saw him in his glorious pomp as the pivot of both the Welsh Grand Slam and victorious Lions sides.

The fans' favourite: Barry's magnetism on the field was matched by a winning persona off it. During the New Zealand Lions tour he was rested for the game against Manawatu. But his box-office appeal was so great this omission left a female pensioner fuming. She wrote him a letter of complaint outlining how she'd saved up especially to see him play. Barry made a surprise visit to the old lady to apologise in person and ended up being greeted by an entire street party.

The King Abdicates: On his return from the 71 Lions tour, Barry attempted to resume his working, family and rugby life under siege from an ever-growing fan base. Autograph hunters gawped through his windows and made giggling phone calls to his home number. Invitations to be lauded at all manner of social events arrived by the sack load.

A visit to Rhyl to open a branch of Midland Bank brought an uncomfortable epiphany. Introduced to The King, a young female member of staff actually curtsied. Feeling his pleasure in the game evaporating with the ever more surreal attention off the field, Barry announced his retirement in a £7000 exclusive for the *Sunday Mirror* in April 1972.

Retiring, he said, was his only escape.

The final farewell: Barry said goodbye to international rugby with a 20–6 victory over France at the Arms Park on March 25, 1972 – not that the watching crowds knew then that The King was abdicating. His last appearance on a rugby field came the following month in a game between a star-studded Barry John XV and an equally impressive side selected by Carwyn James to celebrate the 50th anniversary of Urdd Gobaith Cymru.

Clubs: Cardiff, Llanelli, Cefneithin, Barbarians

TOP TEAM
The Welsh Lions of 1971

In 1971 a British and Irish Lions side defeated the mighty All Blacks in their own backyard. A Test series victory against New Zealand had never been achieved before and it hasn't been done since. And perhaps it might not have happened in 1971 were it not for the Welsh dragons who helped the British Lions roar.

The ultimate Test: captains Meads and Dawes step out at Eden Park, Auckland.

It was the year that saw Britain go decimal, Thatcher snatch school milk away and Idi Amin seize power in Uganda. In the cinemas women wept over *Love Story*, on our TV screens the Two Ronnies made their debut... and on the rugby field Wales ruled supreme. So when the British Lions set off in May 1971, they had 13 of the Welsh Grand Slam team in their midst, not to mention rugby visionary Carwyn James as coach and John Dawes as captain.

Few believed the Lions would actually win, however; indeed the New Zealand press said as much, particularly after their disastrous stop-over in Australia en route, where, jetlagged, they lost to Queensland.

So when Doug Smith, the charismatic Scottish team manager, turned soothsayer on the eve of the first match, prophesying the Lions would take the series with two wins, one loss and a draw, New Zealand deemed his crystal ball as cloudy as a wet day in Invercargill. Four months later, as Smith's prophecy was fulfilled, the All Blacks' glowering captain Colin Meads declared him to be 'the greatest bloody predictor of all time'.

As the Lions embarked on an unbeaten run

Bigger than the Beatles, the 1971 Lions arrive back in Heathrow, led by manager Doug Smith. (*PA Images*)

of provincial matches, New Zealand began to realise they might have been a bit hasty writing the tourists off. 'The biggest fascination of all was that we were winning,' remembers Barry John. 'Suddenly we came to the Wellington game and this was really the crunch. They were full of All Blacks, former All Blacks and top youngsters and we smashed them 47–9. John Bevan scored four tries, I chipped in with the odd point or two. Suddenly New Zealand woke up and realised these boys could play. It was fantastic. From then on it was like an unstoppable train gathering speed.'

Canterbury tried to derail the Lions Express. Provincial sides see it as their patriotic duty to soften up the tourists in time for the Tests but Canterbury stooped to brutal depths in what became known as The Game of Shame.

'It was a rough, violent game,' says Gerald Davies. 'The players complained to the referee within 10 minutes about the punch-ups going on but he said "Whatever happens behind my back is not my responsibility"… It was a brutal game which cost us dearly in terms of playing personnel.'

Victory in the first Test in Dunedin was achieved against the odds. The Lions survived an All Black onslaught but heroic defence and the brilliance of Barry John the Boot sealed the win. It was a result that shook New Zealand to its core.

In the second Test the Lions faced the inevitable All Black backlash, including a fabulous try from New Zealand's star flanker Ian Kirkpatrick. Yet although the Lions lost 22–12 Carwyn James was encouraged enough by the way his team rallied in the second half to believe the series was still there for the taking. And before the crucial third Test the Lions continued to dazzle in the provincial games. When Hawkes Bay tried to turn the game into another mini-Canterbury, the Lions simply turned on the style – four tries from Gerald Davies and a cheeky riposte from Barry John. Taking the ball on his own 25-yard line he put

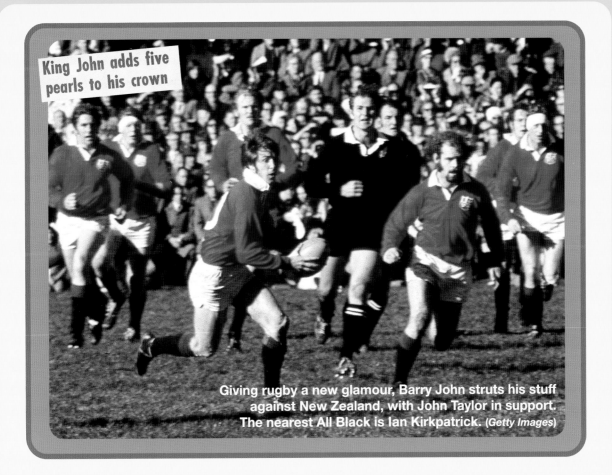

King John adds five pearls to his crown

Giving rugby a new glamour, Barry John struts his stuff against New Zealand, with John Taylor in support. The nearest All Black is Ian Kirkpatrick. (*Getty Images*)

it on the ground, sat on it, waited for the Kiwis to get within reach and then kicked it 50 yards down field.

It was just one of the moments that crowned Barry John king in the land of the long white cloud. The New Zealand public was fascinated by the fly-half's ethereal brilliance, not to mention the way he gave rugby a new glamour.

For Barry John, the third Test encapsulates the 71 Lions experience. The player famed for his nonchalance was feeling the heat: 'This was the shoot-out of shoot-outs… That game was the first time I have felt pressure before a rugby match. It began to dawn on me, as thousands of British fans arrived for the game, just what was being expected of us – and of me in particular.

'For the first 20 minutes of the match, we played brilliant rugby. Gareth Edwards played as well during that period as at any time in his career as we went 13–0 up. After that we were

never going to lose. And we made sure we drew the fourth and final Test to ensure we left New Zealand with a 2–1 victory under our belts. The tour changed attitudes in Britain towards rugby. It was the first time we had knocked football off the back pages.'

At Heathrow, five thousand supporters mobbed the returning rugby tourists. Two lines of fans formed a triumphal arch as the team came off the plane and were tunnelled towards their families.

'The reception was absolutely sensational,' remembers John Taylor, the London Welsh flanker/tour conductor who supplemented his dynamic performances on the pitch

JOHN TAYLOR

with keeping team-mates pitch-perfect in their renditions of 'Sloop John B'. 'I thought the Beatles must be arriving at the same time but the thousands were all for us! Brilliant.'

The party didn't end there. The entire population of Gwaen-cae-Gurwen turned out to cheer Gareth Edwards home. A motorcade of 50 cars and a police escort accompanied his vintage car on the 12-mile journey from the station. Similar scenes of civic pride hailed other Welsh Lions home, while Carwyn James was met by a welcoming committee that included Plaid Cymru leader Gwynfor Evans and folk icon Dafydd Iwan. The Lions became the first rugby team to enter 10 Downing Street as Edward Heath hosted a reception to celebrate their success and they won Team of the Year at the BBC Sports Personality Awards.

The legacy of the 71 Lions tour which saw the Welsh dragons roar is considerable. John Taylor describes it as the 'massive turning point' that finally banished British rugby's inferiority complex. Gerald Davies agrees: 'Beating the best team in the world – beating New Zealand in New Zealand – gave you the feeling there was no obstacle that could not be overcome'.

Front row: J. Taylor, D. Quinnell, C. M. H. Gibson, W. J. McBride, S. J. Dawes (captain), Dr D. C. W. Smith (manager), Carwyn R. James (assistant manager and coach), W. D. Thomas, R.J. McLoughlin, R. Hopkins, J. F. Lynch. Middle row: G. O. Edwards, T. G. R. Davies, J. McLauchlan, R. B. Hiller, J. S. Spencer, B. John, J. V. Pullin, D. J. Duckham, J. P. R. Williams, C. W. W. Rea. Back row: J. F. Slattery, A. Lewis, A. B. Carmichael, P. J. Dixon, A. G. Biggar, G. L. Brown, T. M. Davies, M. G. Roberts, M. L. Hipwell, J. C. Bevan, F. A. L. Laidlaw.

OFFICIAL PHOTOGRAPH OF THE BRITISH LIONS – 1971 NZ TOUR

An 8 O'CLOCK Souvenir

Produced in association with
AIR NEW ZEALAND
In the interest of Rugby

Carwyn James, visionary coach of the 1971 Lions and of the Llanelli team who beat the All Blacks the following year.

253 proves too big a number for Phil Bennett. The All Black digits are (left to right) Tane Norton, Peter Whiting and Keith Murdoch.

Barbarians, Saucepans and Songs (1972–73)

2

1972

This year was a devastating flashpoint in the volatile politics of Northern Ireland.

1972 saw Bloody Sunday which claimed 14 lives, the IRA attack on Aldershot barracks which killed five women and an army priest, and the torching of the British Embassy in Dublin by furious demonstrators.

The repercussions reached sport. Ahead of the Five Nations, letters threatening the safety of teams and their supporters were sent to the unions of England, Scotland and Wales and individual players. England still played Ireland at home but, despite assurances from the IRFU that security would be paramount, Scotland and Wales did not take the risk of travelling to Dublin.

Given that they were unbeaten in their remaining fixtures, there has been speculation that Wales might have achieved back-to-back Grand Slams if the tournament had not been disrupted in 1972.

Barry John

Victory against France in their final game brought Wales their eighth consecutive championship win. It was a match of hellos and goodbyes. Derek Quinnell – capped for the Lions before his country – announced himself to the Five Nations in suitably impatient style, thundering through the tunnel and knocking down half of South Wales Police in his eagerness to take the field as a replacement for an injured Mervyn Davies.

And, though his adoring fans had no idea at the time, it was an international farewell to Barry John who would announce his retirement at just 27 the following month.

All Blacks give Wales the blues

Matches between Wales and New Zealand always seem to produce a controversy that will be spoken of with bitter regret for decades hence. The All Blacks' December visit to Cardiff was no exception. New Zealand may have finally achieved karma for their 1905 defeat with this 19–16 win.

In the Edwardian match, Bob Deans's try for New Zealand was disallowed. In 1972, JPR met a similar fate with his score 15 minutes from time deemed by English referee 'Johnny' Johnson to be a wriggle over rather than a momentum try. The furious full-back protested that his move was exactly the same as the one that had taken prop Keith Murdoch over the line for the All Blacks' only try.

Wales could still have drawn the game – which would have been a fair reflection of the contest. But Phil Bennett missed the last penalty of the match and had to be content that season with defeating the All Blacks in the Scarlet of Llanelli rather than the red of Wales.

A little lower than the Angel, New Zealand's disgraced prop forward Keith Murdoch.

Tony Lewis, Wales and England.

RICHARD BURTON · ELIZABETH TAYLOR
PETER O'TOOLE

DYLAN THOMAS'

UNDER MILK WOOD.

SCREENPLAY & DIRECTION
ANDREW SINCLAIR

GUEST STARS IN ALPHABETICAL ORDER
GLYNIS JOHNS · VIVIEN MERCHANT · SIAN PHILLIPS
COLOUR BY TECHNICOLOR®

Richard Meade

Olympic Golds: 3
Total Medals: 3
First Medal: 1968
Height (cm): 183
Games: 4

A crushed Clive Rowlands commented after the match: 'We should have won. It is the biggest disappointment I have ever had.' The controversies didn't stop at the final whistle. Try-scorer Keith Murdoch morphed from hero to villain when an altercation with an Angel Hotel security guard saw him sent home in disgrace within 24 hours.

In what remains one of rugby's most surreal incidents, however, Murdoch exited the plane in Australia and disappeared into the outback, never to be seen again for many years.

Also in 1972: The face of British shopping was changed forever as French retail giants Carrefour launched the UK's first ever hypermarket in Caerphilly. A revamped Rhoose Airport was opened by the Duke of Edinburgh, while Richard Burton released his film version of *Under Milk Wood* – starring Elizabeth Taylor, Peter O'Toole and half the population of Fishguard. Tony Lewis captained England on his Test debut against India in Delhi, showjumper Richard Meade crowned a gold-medal winning Olympic year with the Welsh Sports Personality of the Year title and John Dawes was made an OBE.

PHIL BENNETT

Phil Bennett was born in Felinfoel – the place that gave the world the innovation of canned beer in 1935. But if we were to look for an appropriate metaphor for one of Wales's greatest fly-halves, Phil was more bottle of pop than can of ale. He fizzed and sparkled as he shimmied through defenders with blistering pace.

Quick-witted with soft hands and fleet feet, he could also torment the opposition with sweetly struck penalties and spiralling kicks to touch that pinned them back deep in their own half.

Accused of lack of confidence in his early career, he ended it with the poise of a triumphant Grand Slam captain and as the world-record holder for the most points scored in internationals.

A debut for the records books: Phil made history with his first cap as he became the first replacement in Welsh rugby history, coming off the bench for an injured Gerald Davies against France in 1969. As substitute wing, he almost didn't make it on to the field when the zip got stuck on his tracksuit but thankfully Norman Gale whipped it off for him. And after all that, he never actually touched the ball.

Decisions, decisions: As a teenager Phil turned down a scholarship to Llandovery College offered by Carwyn James, who had witnessed his talent in a schools tournament. But the youngster whose father had suffered an industrial accident and whose mother was consequently now employed in a factory to make ends meet felt he had to pull his weight at home by starting work rather than staying in school.

A bigger regret was not pursuing the path of a professional footballer – Phil was a Colt with Swansea Town and was invited for trials with West Ham. He also played five games for Aberavon aged 18 before committing to the Scarlets for the rest of his rugby life.

THE STATS Wales: **29** Caps   British & Irish Lions: **8** Caps

The King is dead…long live the King: Barry John's premature departure in 1972 left big boots to fill but although Phil's style could not have been more different from his predecessor he would make the no. 10 shirt emphatically his own.

That's not to say The Big Five Welsh selection panel were always convinced. Despite his dazzling displays on the 74 Lions tour to South Africa, he was controversially dropped in 1975 for John Bevan and considered third choice fly-half behind Bevan and Swansea's David Richards the following season.

Carwyn James summed up the incredulous reaction of many: 'Phil Bennett is the best fly-half in the world. He has flair and style and that little bit of extra God-given skill. To discard Bennett is altogether unbelievable.'

But then both Bevan (elbow) and Richards (hamstring) were injured and Phil was back at no. 10. The twist in the tale inspired a new Max Boyce ditty called – what else? – 'Divine Intervention'.

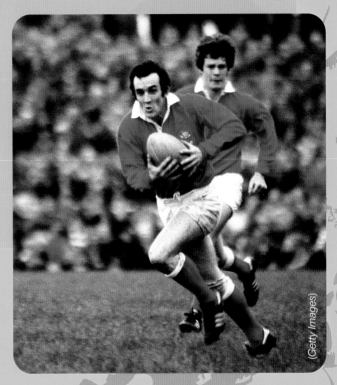
(Getty Images)

Captain Bennett and the best team talk ever: In 1977 Phil took over the Welsh captaincy, succeeding Mervyn Davies whose career had been tragically cut short by a brain haemorrhage the previous year.

He was an inspiring skipper in deeds and words. Indeed his words before the England game that season have gone down in folklore as the fieriest team talk in Welsh dressing room history as he saw Wales v England as 800 years of oppression squeezed into 80 minutes of rugby: 'Look what these bastards have done to Wales. They've taken our coal, our water, our steel. They buy our houses and only live in them for a fortnight every 12 months. What have they given us? Absolutely nothing. We've been exploited, raped, controlled and punished by the English and that's who you are playing this afternoon.' It worked a treat. Wales won 14-9.

A Grand Slam finish: Phil steered his side to the third Welsh Grand Slam of the decade through a brutal match against Ireland and an intense finale against France in which the fly-half scored the decisive try himself.

Far too modest to big up his own legend, Phil Bennett's quicksilver gifts were underlined by a great Welsh no. 10 of an earlier vintage. According to Cliff Morgan the fly-half from Felinfoel 'made the game so exciting you'd have paid an extra £10 on the gate if you knew he was going to be playing.'

Clubs: Llanelli, Aberavon, Felinfoel, Barbarians

TOP TEAM
Llanelli and the All Blacks 1972

1970s teenage heart-throb, David Cassidy.
(*PA Images*)

The doe-eyed face of David Cassidy adorned almost every teenage girl's bedroom in the land in 1972 as he crooned his Partridge Family chart-topper *Point Me In The Direction of Albuquerque*. But this was the year when all of west Wales made a beeline for Llanelli.

As Max Boyce declaimed:

Twas on a dark and dismal day, in a week that had seen rain.
When all roads led to Stradey Park with the All Blacks here again.
They poured down from the Valleys, they came from far and wide.
There were 20,000 in the ground. And me and Dai outside.

These were the opening lines of 9–3 – the poem that captured the greatest moment in Llanelli RFC's history and the club rugby match of the decade.

By the time Ian Kirkpatrick's All Blacks arrived on British soil for their 1972–3 tour the Scarlets had strengthened an already impressive side with star quality from other clubs. J.J. Williams had winged in from Bridgend, Tommy David arrived from Pontypridd to take his place in the back row while Ray 'Chico' Hopkins came from Maesteg to slot in at scrum-half.

But perhaps Llanelli's greatest weapon wasn't even on the field. In their philosopher king coach Carwyn James they had the perfect man to mentor them to victory. He had already shown the British Lions how to beat New Zealand the previous year.

The man who put the three in 9–3, New Zealand's Joe Karam tries to open up Llanelli at Stradey Park. His Scarlet pursuers are (from l. to r.) Ray Gravell, Andy Hill, Phil Bennett and J.J. Williams.

Before the players ran out in front of a capacity crowd, Carwyn implored them to 'Think about it, think about it, think about it – it's a thinking game.'

If their coach appealed to their heads, their captain stirred their hearts. Delme Thomas – after his usual pre-match delicacy of raw eggs and sherry – galvanised the Stradey dressing room with an inspirational team talk. The veteran of three Lions tours, a Welsh Grand Slam, and 25 international caps told his men he would 'give it all away just to win this game today.'

It was a speech that left Ray Gravell and Phil Bennett in tears while young flanker and future Welsh coach Gareth Jenkins was ready to run through the dressing room wall. Then there was Roy 'Shunto' Thomas, who burned with let-me-at-em fervour.

'We was on fire like. Marvellous!' beamed the former steelworker. 'And we wouldn't let him down. We wouldn't let him down'. And he didn't, although coach Carwyn James wasn't very impressed with the hooker's response

to the haka. 'I gave them a clap. Carwyn said "What were you doing? You're not supposed to clap the haka!"'

But that was the last bit of respect Llanelli paid New Zealand, puncturing their aura of invincibility by taking an early lead and refusing to surrender in the face of some truly thuggish rugby from the men in black.

The only try of the game was scored within three minutes of kick-off. A curving penalty from Phil Bennett bounced off the cross-bar. As All-Black scrum-half Lin Colling attempted a rather leisurely clearance kick, Scarlets centre Roy Bergiers pounced with a charge-down, diving on the ball for the try.

It wasn't the most glamorous of scores but it was enough to give Llanelli a lead they never relinquished. A penalty from All Black full-back Joe Karam left it at 6–3 by the break but penalties from Phil Bennett and Andy Hill in the second half stretched the Scarlets' lead to that iconic 9–3 scoreline.

It was a torrid encounter that saw some fearsome rucking from the All Blacks, not to mention several fights. But roared on by every inhabitant of Llanelli the home side would not lie down, nullifying the All Black threat up front so their backs could not cut loose, and defending as if their lives depended on it.

As Delme Thomas would later tell the *Western Mail*: 'We squeezed them and never let them go.' The *New Zealand Herald*, meanwhile, admitted 'the better team, by a long, long margin, won the game. The All Blacks were out thought and out fought.'

The town celebrated this historic victory with positively Bacchanalian carnage. It was indeed 'the day the pubs ran dry'.

Among the thousands who shared the joy of the day the Scarlets painted the town red was a young Huw Edwards. He may now occupy the hottest seat in BBC news but in 1972 he also had the best seat in Stradey Park – even if he had to bring it with him.

'I was among a group of Llanelli Grammar schoolboys on the touchline when Llanelli beat the All Blacks in that stupendous game,' he recalled. 'I was 11 years old. We paid 5p to see the match and carried gym benches across to Stradey Park to provide extra seating. I still have vivid memories of Delme Thomas being carried shoulder-high after the 9-3 win.'

The recollections endure because the deeds of Carwyn James's men have seeped into song and verse like the battle triumphs of medieval knights. The lyrics of David Cassidy may not have lasted but no modern rendering of the Scarlets' anthem is complete without the 1972 amendment: 'Who beat the All Blacks, but good old Sosban Fach?'

And let's not forget the final words of Boyce the Bard in *9–3*:

> And when I'm old and my hair turns grey
>   and they put me in the chair,
> I'll tell my great-grandchildren that their
>   Datcu was there.
> And they'll ask to hear the story of that damp
>   October day,
> when I went down to Stradey and I saw the
>   Scarlets play.

'Who beat the All Blacks?' No. 10 Phil Bennett knows the answer, whilst New Zealand skipper Ian Kirkpatrick (right) and Lindsay Colling refuse to believe it.

1973 – A Bit of a Blip

It had never happened before and it will never happen again. But in 1973, as each nation won their two home fixtures and lost their two away games, the Five Nations championship was shared between all five teams.

Wales's favourites status had been enhanced by their imperious five-try defeat of England in their opening game. It was a performance that had former player turned rugby scribe Clem Thomas purring: 'It is difficult to find superlatives to extol fully the virtues, the efficiency and the creativity of the Welsh backs.'

Yet it was the superiority of the Scottish forwards that saw Wales mugged at Murrayfield in their following game. Fierce Caledonian defence nullified the stellar Welsh backline. And as Wales failed to score a try for the first time in 10 years, they conceded two in the first half.

Their run of nine consecutive championship wins had stuttered to a halt. But they bounced back to defeat a stubborn and spirited Ireland in Cardiff and still had a chance of championship glory against France in Paris. Welsh fans dared to dream as Les Bleus made 10 changes after their loss to England. Yet only France could jettison practically their entire backline and still produce the goods, tackling the Welsh attackers out of the game. Four missed penalties also cost Wales dear.

MERVYN DAVIES

It wasn't all about the backs… Mervyn Davies about to give England's John Watkins something to think about at Cardiff.

THAT GAME. THAT TRY.
That Fellow Edwards.

Gareth Edwards

If Wales's uneven progress through the 1973 Five Nations was disappointing, supporters could still savour the Cymric contribution to a game that will resonate in rugby folklore forever.

Guided by Carwyn James and glittering with Welsh star quality, the 1973 Barbarians met the All Blacks in Cardiff and produced arguably the most entertaining match of the 20th century.

The iconic highlight of the game had a commentary to match from a Welsh legend from an earlier golden age – Cliff Morgan. Here's how his words and their actions unfolded…

'This is great stuff. Phil Bennett covering': New Zealand right wing Bryan Williams must still rue the day he sent a kick deep into the Baabaas 22 for Bennett to collect. Perhaps he thought the Welsh fly-half would boot it back but our Phil was in the mood for a dance…

'Chased by Alistair Scown': The Kiwi flanker was indeed on Bennett's tail. And he wasn't the only one.

'Brilliant! Oh that's brilliant!': Not even Houdini could have escaped the encroaching All Black defence. But Houdini couldn't jink like Phil Bennett, who sidestepped four players and shimmied out of danger to send the ball to…

'John Williams': As this was pre-JJ, also a John Williams, JPR hadn't yet been reduced to the initials the world would henceforth know him by.

'Bryan Williams': This challenge would be a straight yellow-card these days but thankfully

Barbarians at the West Gate: (from l. to r.) Tom David, John Pullin, John Dawes, Gareth Edwards, scorer of 'That Try', and Derek Quinnell. Meanwhile, Sid Going (no. 9) has his work cut out.

for rugby posterity JPR shrugged off his namesake's high tackle and kept the ball – and the greatest try ever – alive. Even though, in Gareth Edwards's words: 'He was virtually decapitated'.

'Pullin': The English captain – and the only non-Welshman in the move – received JPR's pass with perfect timing and delivered it to…

'John Dawes. Great dummy': Was it a dummy? 'If Cliff Morgan says it was a dummy, it was a dummy,' laughed Dawes. 'It was one of those things. John Bevan was running up outside me but I could see he was covered, so the ball had to go back inside me.' Where he found flanker…

'David. Tom David': 'John Dawes made my career with that pass,' recalled the uncapped player who was a late replacement for a flu-ridden Mervyn Davies. 'I was just a boy from Pontypridd, had never played for Wales and this was the biggest game of my life.'

'The halfway line': And the Baa Baas are still flying through the All Black defence… with both Gareth Edwards and John Bevan tracking the move in the hope of a scoring pass. But the forwards want to share in the fun…

'Brilliant by Quinnell': It almost breaks down but Derek swoops for the ball off his bootlaces and, hearing Gareth Edwards hollering: 'Give it here!' in Welsh, sends a flat pass in the direction of the scrum-half.

'This is Gareth Edwards! A dramatic start! What a score! Oh that fellow Edwards! Who can stop a man like that!' The All Blacks looked as if they were expecting John Bevan to take the scoring pass but the surprise element was Gareth arriving to collect the ball at full pelt. He later admitted he had 'never run so fast on a rugby pitch'.

'If the greatest writer of the written word would have written that story no-one would have believed it.' Absolutely – and the rugby world has enjoyed retelling the tale of That Try by That Fellow Edwards ever since.

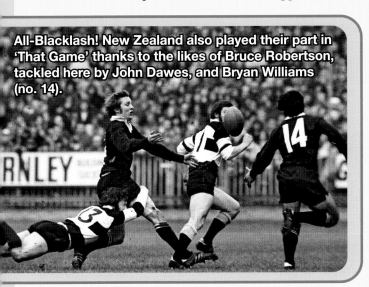

All-Blacklash! New Zealand also played their part in 'That Game' thanks to the likes of Bruce Robertson, tackled here by John Dawes, and Bryan Williams (no. 14).

Also in 1973: Max Boyce created the quintessential rugby LP, recording *Live At Treorchy*. It could have been *Live At Penygraig* but, conceding that their function room was too small, the mid-Rhondda club magnanimously sent the game's troubadour further up the valley to their upper-Rhondda rivals. Penygraig still created rugby history that year, however, hosting Japan's first ever game in Wales. The Far East connection continued in Bridgend, where Sony opened its Welsh factory.

Karl Jenkins won British Jazz Album of the Year with *Soft Machine Six* while Philip Madoc made a memorable appearance as a U-boat captain in *Dad's Army* – 'Don't tell him Pike!' Hurdler Berwyn Price won Welsh Sports Personality of the Year, while Welsh rugby mourned the death of 94-year-old Willie Llewellyn – the last remaining hero of Wales's 1905 victory over the All Blacks.

MAX BOYCE

If the players were Welsh sporting royalty, the bard at the court of rugby in the 70s was Max Boyce. As he reflected their legendary deeds on the field in comedy, poetry and song, the entertainer from Glynneath helped create a new kind of Welsh rugby fan culture.

From popularising the chant of 'Oggie! Oggie! Oggie!' to coining the catchphrase 'I Was There' to the penning of Wales's second anthem 'Hymns and Arias', Max was the ultimate 16th Man.

The former miner recorded a changing Wales, where rugby success was a welcome distraction from the decline of heavy industry. Max reflected the laughter and sadness of close-knit communities adapting to this new world – and how Wales clung to rugby as a signifier of national identity that still endured.

Live At Treorchy

The LP which would find its way into every Welsh rugby fan's record collection was *Live At Treorchy*, and it was the album which changed Max's life, allowing him to give up the day job in Neath's Metal Box factory and launch a showbiz career spanning 40 years and two million record sales.

Recorded in Treorchy Rugby Club in the Rhondda on November 23, 1973, this compilation of stand-up, song and verse astonished the music industry by staying in the album charts for 38 weeks, turning gold and attracting fans from Murrayfield to Melbourne.

Hymns and Arias

Every album has its greatest hit of course. *Live At Treorchy's* has to be 'Hymns and Arias', the hilarious tale of a weekend in 'Twickers' which is now sung wherever Welsh rugby is played all over the world. Yet back in 1973 this people's anthem was barely known to an audience of Treorchy locals, many of whom had to be coerced into coming.

At the time the up-and-coming performer wasn't exactly a hot ticket. 'We couldn't sell the tickets because they hadn't heard of me,' Max recalls. 'And they were only 50p. We ended up giving them away. They came because they almost felt sorry for me so it was remarkable really!'

Hymns and Arias

We paid our weekly shilling for that January trip:
A long weekend in London, aye, without a bit of kip.
There's a seat reserved for beer by the boys from Abercarn:
There's beer, pontoon, crisps and fags and a croakin' Calon Lân.

chorus
And we were singing hymns and arias,
Land of my Fathers, Ar Hyd y Nos.

Into Paddington we did roll with an empty crate of ale.
Will had lost at cards and now his Western Mail's for sale.
But Will is very happy though his money all has gone:
He swapped five photos of his wife for one of Barry John.

We got to Twickers early and were jostled in the crowd;
Planted leeks and dragons, looked for toilets all around.
So many there we couldn't budge – twisted legs and pale:
I'm ashamed we used a bottle that once held bitter ale.

Wales defeated England in a fast and open game.
We sang Cwm Rhondda and Delilah,
Damn, they sounded both the same.
We sympathised with an Englishman
Whose team was doomed to fail
So we gave him that old bottle that once held bitter ale!

So it's down to Soho for the night,
To the girls with the shiny beads;
To the funny men with lipstick on,
With evil minds and deeds.
One said to Will from a doorway dark,
Damn, she didn't have much on.
But Will knew what she wanted,
Aye... his photo of Barry John!

Cos she was singing hymns and arias,
Land of my Fathers, Ar hyd y nos.

We All Had Doctor's Papers

A word-of-mouth sensation, *Live At Treorchy* may have relied on Welsh humour and pathos for its content but it struck a chord across Britain, selling by the box-load. Max's follow up album – *We All Had Doctor's Papers* – became the first and only comedy LP to top the UK album charts, reaching number one in the summer of 1975 ahead of Pink Floyd, Wings, Elton John and Rod Stewart.

(BBC)

Icon

But if 'Hymns and Arias' has become a second Welsh anthem, *Live At Treorchy* has become an icon of Welsh popular culture. In the words of historian Martin Johnes: 'It is as important to an understanding of Welshness as anything Dylan Thomas or Saunders Lewis wrote.'

And Max Boyce is as important to an understanding of Welsh rugby in the 70s as anybody who donned the red jersey in that sensational decade.

1974 debutant, Pontypool flanker Terry Cobner, who would become a central figure in the Welsh Grand Slam packs of 1976 and 1978. (*Colorsport*)

A Spring to Forget, a Summer to Remember (1974)

Wales won a single match that championship season – against Scotland, where flanker Terry Cobner sealed his debut with a try. Though they drew against Ireland and France, Wales still had a chance of winning the Five Nations if they could beat England in Twickenham. But the omens for a dismal afternoon were there before kick-off. The Welsh national anthem was omitted from the build-up leaving furious Welsh fans at HQ to improvise an impromptu acapella version. Despite the Gwlads still floating around the stands the Irish ref John West started the match.

His popularity with the travelling faithful took a further dip when he refused to award J.J. Williams a try – after the winger seemed to win the race to the touchdown with Peter Squires and David Duckham. West hadn't kept up with the pace and said his view of the touchdown was obscured. That match ended with a 16–12 defeat for Wales with only Max Boyce salvaging anything from it in the shape of a new song about blind Irish referees.

The season saw the end of Clive Rowlands' reign as Welsh coach. And despite – by their standards – a very average championship, Wales provided a strong contingent of players on that year's Lions tour to South Africa.

Also in 1974:

The map of Welsh counties was redrawn with the reorganisation of local government, as the old names of Gwent, Dyfed and Powys were given a modern outing. Years of conspiracy theories were sparked with the crash of a 'UFO' in a remote part of North Wales. It became known as 'The Berwyn Mountain Incident'. Barry's Helen Morgan was crowned Miss World… but forced to resign four days later when her unmarried mother status was revealed. Plaid Cymru's Gwynfor Evans lost his Carmarthen seat in the February election by just three votes – but regained it in October with a majority of 3,640. And Windsor Davies appeared as the bellowing sergeant major in *It Ain't Half Hot Mum* for the first time.

Gwynfor Evans
(PA Images)

Player Profile
MERVYN DAVIES

His entry to international rugby was as sudden as his devastating exit. Mervyn Davies was an unknown 22-year-old primary school teacher on his Welsh debut – picked just three months after his first appearance for London Welsh in 1969. By the time his career was cut short by a brain haemorrhage seven years later the no. 8 was lauded as one of the greatest forwards in the world.

Like father like son: Born in Swansea, the elder of two brothers, Mervyn was a multi-talented sportsman, excelling at cricket, football and, as his lanky six-foot three-inch form suggested, basketball. But it was rugby that would dominate by the time he reached his late teens. His father David had played for Wales in the Victory internationals – the non-capped matches staged just after World War II.

From grassroots to the field of dreams: After studying at Swansea College of Education, Mervyn moved to Guildford to start work as a teacher in a Frimley Green primary school. He also joined the local rugby club but soon moved to London Welsh. By the time he had progressed from the thirds to the first XV at Old Deer Park, Wales were calling. He won his first cap alongside fellow debutant J.P.R. Williams against Scotland in 1969.

The headband, the moustache... and that nickname: It wasn't just his lean-bodied brilliance that made Mervyn stand out. As well as his passing finesse, lineout skills and athleticism at the breakdown, he cultivated a distinctive look that gave him an aura of don't-mess-with-me menace.

He restrained his afro-like mop of black hair with his trademark headband while the Spaghetti Western moustache added another cult-hero touch. And there was the nickname. Why was Merve the Swerve so called? The answer lies in his biography where he revealed the young Merve was a mean surfer. Riding the waves of Swansea Bay certainly got those hips swivelling.

THE STATS Wales: **38** Caps British & Irish Lions: **8** Caps

Lion-hearted performances: For the All Blacks, the Welsh no. 8 was the forward who was pivotal to their defeat to the Lions of 71. 'It was not just that Davies achieved domination for the Lions at the back of the lineout,' said Kiwi captain Colin Meads. 'He moved with quite startling speed and intelligence – an instinctive reaction almost – to trouble spots, killing ball till the Lions could regroup.'

He was again the key forward in the Lions 1974 triumph over the Springboks, denying England no. 8 Andy Ripley – also on terrific form – the Test spot.

A tragic end to a brilliant career and a remarkable recovery: Just three weeks after leading Wales to the Grand Slam, 29-year-old Mervyn collapsed with an intra-cranial haemorrhage when captaining Swansea against Pontypool during a Schweppes Cup semi-final at Cardiff Arms Park. He credited his survival that day to the fact there were medics on hand. Physically and mentally, it was a long and difficult journey back to health. Mervyn never played rugby again and struggled with the co-ordination to enjoy other sports like golf and squash.

Awarded an OBE after his recovery, he was eventually able to express his rugby expertise through punditry in print and on air and as an accomplished speaker on the after-dinner circuit.

Grand Slam Captain: The man with the headband was handed the skipper's armband in 1975. He captained Wales to the championship that season and the Grand Slam in 1976. He played with typical lead-from-the-front valour in the Grand Slam decider against France, refusing to leave the field despite the agony of a ripped calf sustained in the opening quarter. Though no-one knew it at the time, this defining performance was his last in a Welsh shirt.

Farewell to a legend: In his early 60s, Mervyn faced another harrowing fight – against the lung cancer that would claim his life in 2012. He died at the age of 65 on the eve of the Wales v France match. Victory brought Wales the Grand Slam – the team cited Mervyn Davies as their inspiration and dedicated their triumph to the player voted the greatest Welsh captain of all time.

Clubs: Swansea, London Welsh, Barbarians

TOP TEAM
The Welsh Lions of 1974

Rising prices were a feature of an inflation-ridden UK in 1974 but there was one place where no British sports fan minded the numbers going up and up – the rugby fields of South Africa.

'Great play, JJ!' Four Welsh Lions celebrate the first of the star winger's two tries during the third Test against the Springboks. (From l. to r.) Phil Bennett, Bobby Windsor, Gareth Edwards and J.J. Williams.

As a rampant Lions side roared from Western Transvaal to Johannesburg, the scoreboard told a remarkable story. Winning 21 consecutive matches and drawing the final Test, Willie John McBride's men racked up a record 729 points.

Their unbeaten campaign saw them score 107 tries and become the first team to triumph over the Springboks in a four-match series for 78 years. Records tumbled in their wake. The biggest win by any touring team came in the form of a 97–0 demolition of South Western Districts with J.J. Williams crossing the whitewash six times to set a new try-scoring record.

JJ was one of nine Welshmen who made a significant impact on that tour – Mervyn Davies, Phil Bennett, Gareth Edwards, J.P.R. Williams, Roy Bergiers, Clive Rees, Tom David and Bobby Windsor.

Should I Go or Should I Stay?

Yet it was a success story clouded by controversy. Should the Lions even have gone to play the white man's game in racially segregated South Africa? The tourists may have received a rapturous welcome home but they had left these shores condemned by the anti-apartheid movement and without the blessing of the British government.

It was a moral issue on which Wales and London Welsh flanker John Taylor was prepared to make a stand. Interviewed at the time, he said: 'After a great deal of thought I now feel that were I to play I would be helping to condone and perhaps perpetuate a government of the kind that is now in existence in South Africa.'

Gerald Davies would also turn the 74 Lions down, outwardly for job and family reasons, inwardly through a discomfort with the regime of segregation he had witnessed at first hand on the 1968 Lions tour.

The pressure on the Lions not to go to South Africa was applied right up to take off. Under siege in their London hotel from anti-apartheid demonstrators led by Peter Hain, any wavering players were given the last-minute option not to board the plane, as Phil Bennett recalls.

'Many politicians didn't want us to go. Many people didn't want us to go. Willie John McBride, my first Lions captain and an absolute legend, said "Men, you've either got to come 100 per cent committed or stay behind here in London. You've got the next 10 minutes to think about it. Either leave the room and I'll think no less or more of you, or stay here and we go together." And he was an incredible inspiration. We made the decision. I made the decision. Whether it was the right one, to this day we will never know.'

Condemned at home and underrated by their hosts, the siege mentality created before a ball

Merve the Swerve, the Verve on the Veldt!
The Welsh no. 8 puts the Lions on the
front foot as South African flanker
Jan Ellis prepares to tackle.

had even been kicked evolved into a formidable team spirit. And Welsh flair would help give the Lions the edge.

Fighting Fire with Fire

Despite such talent, South Africa weren't expecting much from the northern hemisphere's finest. But the Springboks would rue the day they underestimated the Lions.

'They were expecting to smash us as they had done in 1968,' says J.J. Williams. 'They were dying to test their beloved Springboks against us because remember in that country if you are a Springbok you are a god. They thought the Lions were there for the taking. But it wasn't going to be like that. We had changed our attitude. Our management and players like Gareth had been there in 68 and realised what it was all about. They knew if you're going to go into that arena you have to fight fire with fire.'

Those incendiary tactics started in the pack, whose mental and physical power was symbolised by their infamous code word. If you think '99' signifies an ice cream with a flake stuck in it, it's time to brush up on your rugby folklore.

Phil Bennett gives the captain's description: 'What Willie had said was "If I shout '99' we all pile in and hit the nearest Springbok".'

Whilst it might not have been everyone's cup of tea, J.P.R. Williams seemed to relish the official sanctioning of such a robust approach, often running in from full-back to enter the fray. As JPR understood it: 'If everyone laid into the nearest Springbok then no-one could be sent off.'

First Test

The Lions arrived in a damp Cape Town for the first Test with four Welshmen in the backs – JPR, JJ, Gareth Edwards and Phil Bennett – and two in the pack, Bobby Windsor and Mervyn Davies. The Lions set the tone for the Test series from the very first scrum, and the two Welsh forwards would play a pivotal role.

The late Mervyn Davies described how the pitch was a total quagmire: 'This was the first time we'd come up against the strength of South Africa but we totally annihilated them up front. The scrum was so low and in the first scrum, because he couldn't move his legs, Bobby Windsor hooked the ball with his head. It was unbelievable. But the pressure we managed to exert on their eight – the power we could generate – made us feel almost invincible.'

In the Cape Town mud, the Lions forwards roared. Tries were hard to come by in these conditions but Wales's scrum-half Gareth Edwards put a stylish seal on a 12–3 victory with a drop goal. So now the Lion had shown its claws how would the wounded Springbok respond?

Second Test

'The whole country was in turmoil,' remembers J.J. Williams. 'The Springboks locked themselves away for the week, made changes and by the time they came out on the field in Loftus Versfeld they were a bag of nerves. We hit them quickly with two tries – which I scored – and with fast running rugby and quick thinking. And all of a sudden they were lost. They were gone.'

As the Lions forwards crushed their opposing pack, the Lions backs cut loose, with Phil Bennett in particular dazzling that day. The Llanelli fly-half plotted a mazy and mesmerising path to the try line that left them grasping thin air. He was frequently unleashed on the hard grounds of the high veldt by the long pass of Gareth Edwards, who was also enjoying imperious form, darting from the base of the scrum or opting for a perfectly timed kick. The Lions 28–9 triumph was the heaviest defeat ever inflicted on the Boks by the British and Irish tourists.

Third and Fourth Tests

The third Test at Port Elizabeth offered the host nation their last chance to save the series. It would prove a brutal encounter, but it was the Boks who came off worse in the scrapping. They were also second best by a long way in the game itself. JJ enjoyed a brace of tries once more while Phil Bennett sealed the match and the series with a dropped goal that brought the final score to an emphatic 26–9.

The only match the Lions didn't win was the final Test in Johannesburg. But as it was a 13–13 draw, they still remained unbeaten.

Returning Heroes

As in 1971, the Welsh heroes were given a welcome in the hillsides when they returned. Both Phil and JJ were transported by horse and carriage through their communities while hundreds lined the streets.

It wasn't just family and friends giving the Lions a hero's welcome. The politicians were back in on the act, both Edward Heath and Sports Minister Denis Howell lauded their achievements, despite expressing their opposition before the tour.

But had the Lions made their own political statement beyond the field of play? The Springboks were a potent symbol of white supremacy. By crushing them the Lions created a rallying point for black dissent. Initially opposed to the tour, black South Africa followed the humiliation of the Springboks with growing interest.

Those who took part believe, ultimately, they made more impact on South Africa's vile regime by going than staying away, as Gareth Edwards explains: 'Rugby was the game of the Afrikaner, which is why the black people took so much pleasure from our win. It was as if we had delivered a blow on their behalf.'

'Get off my back!' JPR is the Lion trying to shake off his Springbok predator, Jan Ellis.

Joker in the pack
A GROGG

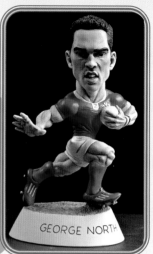

(Courtesy of World of Grogg)

GEORGE NORTH

There is only one way to achieve true immortality in Welsh life. Forget the Gorsedd, the Honours List or even getting your signed picture on the wall of Giovanni's restaurant in Cardiff. You only know you've really made it when you're a Grogg.

Founding father John Hughes was the Michelangelo of rugby and the success of the 70s generation was his muse. As the Welsh game flourished, John peopled mantelpieces across the land with his fabulous rugby figurines.

It all began in a coal-shed in the Hughes' back garden in Treforest, where his first creations were giant figures from the Mabinogion. But with more contemporary legends being formed on the field of play, John started to express his love of rugby in clay.

'The team got better and better so I made a few Groggs,' John explained in *Feat of Clay*. 'The breakthrough – for Wales and the Groggs – came when we beat England at the Arms Park in 1969. Roy Mason of the Wales Tourist Board allowed us to put on a display in their windows in Castle Street, a spin pass away from the stadium and right next to several pubs and the legendary Angel Hotel.

'On the day of the match thousands of fans must have walked past them. One such fan was Byron James of Energlyn Building, Caerphilly. He bought the lot on the Monday morning! The Groggs were up and running.'

By 1971, the Groggs had found their permanent home in the former Dan-y-Graig pub on the Broadway in Treforest. It would become as much a part of the rugby pilgrim route for fans from across the globe as the Arms Park.

Through the 70s, Groggs of 30 Welsh players were crafted. There were also generic figurines such as Lewis the Leap, Drop Kick Davies and Pushover Pugh.

And as the 'Uglies', as the more roughly-crafted early Groggs were known, spread to living rooms across Wales, we got our first Gareth Edwards. By the time I met Gareth around 20 years later his clay alter ego had lost his nose, chipped his elbow and been relegated to a more lowly spot in my parents' living room.

I still blush at the memory of the opening line I gushed to the greatest player – and most ubiquitous Grogg – of all time: 'You're our doorstop!'

But it just goes to show how the rugby figurines became a well-loved part of the furniture in so many Welsh homes. John died in 2013 aged 78. Today the iconic production line continues through the immense talent of his son Richard. And every modern player knows he hasn't really made it until he's a Grogg.

(Courtesy of World of Grogg)

GRAHAM PRICE BOBBY WINDSOR CHARLIE FAULKNER

THE WELSH FRONT ROW
GRAND SLAM 1976, 1978

(Courtesy of World of Grogg)

The direct and hard-running Steve Fenwick, one of the Class of 75.

Carnage, Sacrilege and a New Age (1975–1976)

The Golden Era shifted into its second phase of greatness in 1975 as Wales began the Five Nations with a new coach (John Dawes); a new captain (Mervyn Davies) and six new caps (props Graham Price and Charlie Faulkner, centres Steve Fenwick and Ray Gravell, fly-half John Bevan and flanker Trevor Evans).

This fresh side couldn't have got off to a better start with a fabulous win in Paris which featured Graham Price galloping from his own half to crown his international debut with a famous try. Victory against England at home followed but John Dawes found himself apologising for a second half in which his players 'went off the boil' after zipping to a 16–0 lead by half time. An 80-minute performance was promised for Murrayfield. 'This is a relatively inexperienced team and we have not seen the best of it yet,' asserted captain Mervyn Davies. 'We all know we'll have to flog our backsides off to beat Scotland at Murrayfield but we'll do it.'

But they didn't. The Welsh daffodil wilted on this St David's Day encounter at Murrayfield in front of a record crowd of 104,000. There was spectator carnage as fans – including an estimated 40,000 from Wales – shoehorned their way in and found they couldn't even see the field. The away support didn't actually miss much as Phil Bennett came on for the injured John Bevan and had a shocker. Allan Martin missed the conversion of Wales's only try – a successful kick would have drawn the game. A chastened Wales returned home while the Scottish Rugby Union announced all future matches would be all-ticket with a capacity of just over 70,000.

Even more direct and hard-running, the formidable and lovable Ray Gravell.

Phil Bennett redeemed himself with a stunning display that helped take Ireland apart a fortnight later in Cardiff. The 32–4 triumph brought Wales the Five Nations championship and Ireland its worst championship scoreline for 68 years.

The dragon breathes fires in the Land of the Rising Sun and wallops the Wallabies

A scorching September spent on tour in Japan saw Wales blistering in attack as temperatures climbed to almost 90F. They scored 45 tries in five games, conceding only one against the Japan B side. And while their opponents were never going to be formidable, the tour proved a successful bonding enterprise as the recent caps and established stars became a tight unit.

Australia were certainly taught a lesson by the exciting Class of 75. On a crisp sunlight afternoon five days before Christmas the visiting Wallabies were dispatched 28–3. In one of his finest games for Wales, J.J. Williams – playing on his favoured right wing – scored a stylish hat-trick. The second half of the Golden Era was starting to glisten.

Another 1975 new boy, outside half John Bevan, looks for support against Australia – and it's on its way in the shape of (from l. to r.) Trevor Evans, Charlie Faulkner, Allan Martin and Graham Price.

Also in 1975: Max Boyce released *We All Had Doctors Papers*. Angharad Rees starred in the hit drama of the year *Poldark*. Ryan and Ronnie, meanwhile, announced the end of their comedy partnership. The Welsh football team qualified for the quarter-finals of the 1976 European Championship and snooker's Ray Reardon became world champion for the fourth time.

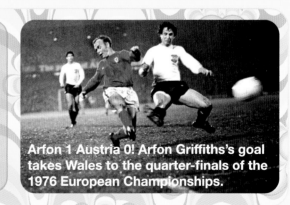

Arfon 1 Austria 0! Arfon Griffiths's goal takes Wales to the quarter-finals of the 1976 European Championships.

1976

The season began with what many considered an act of sacrilege – Phil Bennett was dropped from the Welsh squad ahead of their opening game at Twickenham. Newspaper headlines demanded The Big Five – Wales's all-powerful quintet of selectors – should be sacked and replaced with a single supremo. Former Llanelli captain Handel Greville said: 'Surely nobody in his right senses would say, as the selectors did, that John Bevan and David Richards are better fly-halves than Bennett at the moment.'

Bennett himself revealed: 'What has hurt most is the fact that I was considered the number one fly-half for the Wales game against Australia but now find myself a nonentity.'

But, lo and behold, injuries to both Bevan and Richards meant Bennett was back in after all – and he was never dropped again. He more than proved his worth in a record 21–9 win at Twickenham in which JPR maintained his warrior reputation against England by scoring two tries.

The following game against Scotland also had its share of off-field controversy as the players were banned from giving interviews in the build-up. The Welsh press called it The Great Gag Match. While The Big Five reckoned they were protecting the players everyone else speculated they were vicariously safeguarding themselves, still stung by the criticism they faced for the fiasco of Bennett's omission. The emphatic 28–6 defeat of England is remembered for Bennett becoming Wales's highest points scorer (92); Gareth Edwards equalling Ken Jones's try scoring record (17) and 50-year-old French ref Andre limping through the game after refusing to leave the field when he injured his calf in a collision.

Slippery as a salmon, Gareth Edwards eludes Mike Lampkowski's grasp to score at Twickenham.

A darker build-up shadowed the game against Ireland in Dublin. But despite several Welsh players receiving death threats purporting to be from terrorist extremists, Wales crossed the Irish Sea and shared the Shelbourne Hotel with their opponents, guarded by heavy security.

On the field they enjoyed complete freedom, scoring four tries – three of which arrived in a five-minute onslaught – to record their highest total against Ireland, capturing the Triple Crown in the process.

Now only France in Cardiff stood in the way of the Grand Slam. Les Bleus had an inspirational captain in the diminutive 5ft 5ins form of Jacques Fouroux, aka the 'Little Napoleon'. But Wales had a talismanic skipper too in Mervyn Davies. And that day he led with immense character in what would sadly prove to be his last outing in the red of Wales.

Just minutes into the match the no. 8 was trampled by the French pack and in agony as they punctured his calf muscle with their studs. But refusing to exit the stage, he gave himself no option but to play through the pain.

He steered his men through a torrid battle in which a supercharged France threw everything at the Welsh defence. But the indomitable attitude of the Slam-chasing side was embodied in JPR's try-saving shoulder-charge that barged winger Jean-François Gourdon into touch. The nation

'Wham, bam, our Grand Slam!' JPR's famous shoulder charge on Jean-François Gourdon.

raised its arms as the full-back fist-pumped the air at a challenge he would only have got away with in 1976.

The second Grand Slam of the decade was secured with a record 102 points. But there would be a desperately poignant postscript to the campaign. Just three weeks later, in a Schweppes Cup semi-final tie between Swansea and Pontypool on the club ground next door, Mervyn Davies collapsed with a brain haemorrhage. Following brain surgery he made a remarkable recovery but this true Welsh great would never grace a rugby field again.

The Pain de Galles! France were Wales's greatest rivals in the 1970s, and always had ferocious forwards, like (from l. to r.) Alain Paco, Robert Paparemborde, Michel Palmie (no. 5), Jean-Francois Imbernon (with headband), Gerard Cholley (with ball), Jean-Pierre Rives and Jean-Pierre Bastiat. Their Napoleon in 1976, however, was no. 9 Jacques Fouroux.

In 1976, unlike the Welsh rugby team, singer Bonnie Tyler was lost in France! (*PA Images*)

Bonnie Tyler
LOST IN FRANCE
Top Hit
England
RCA
Baby I Remember You

Phew, what a scorcher!

Nigel Williams

BRITAIN'S 79-year-old temperature record was broken yesterday when Cheltenham and the village of Nailstone in Leicestershire recorded highs of nearly 99F.

The precise measurements made Cheltenham slightly hotter at 98.8F (37.1C), compared with Nailstone's 98.6 (37C). Bar-sourne in Worcestershire was 98F (36.7C), equal to the...

As the heatwave broke local records across the country, pollution levels were also rising to record levels. Ground-level ozone concentrations in areas of southern England were set to be the highest since the summer of 1976.

At Yarner Wood in Devon the maximum hourly concentration reached 147 parts per billion. The World Health Organisation's guideline maximum values for human health are 75-100 parts per billion over hourly average or 50-60ppb over...

gen oxides and hydrocarbons produced by car exhaust, highly reactive and quickly appears in buildings, and it broken down by the nitric oxide which helps in its formation, a spokeswoman for National Society for Clean Air in Brighton said.

Heat exhaustion among District walkers led to several call-outs for the Langdale Ambleside mountain rescue team. Stuart Hulse, leader of the team, said people have been out without enough food and water.

Almost 100 square miles of moorland in the Peak District...

The best year of our lives.. 1976
WHY IT WAS A GREAT TIME TO BE YOUNG

Also in 1976: Rhondda-born actor and avid rugby fan Stanley Baker was knighted in May just a few months before his death. Wales basked in the heatwave summer of 76. High-speed rail travel arrived as the first Intercity 125 trains ran between Swansea and London Paddington. Prince Charles was challenged by miners' leader Dai Francis in the election for Chancellor of the University of Wales. And Bonnie Tyler released her debut single 'Lost in France'.

Player Profile
J.P.R. WILLIAMS

Arguably the most famous full-back in Welsh rugby history, John Peter Rhys Williams began his career as a nipper with Trelales Primary Under 11s and ended it as a veteran 40 years later with Tondu Thirds – dazzling in the golden era of Wales and the Lions in between, of course. Here are just some of the reasons why the legend grew bigger than those superb sideburns.

The Ball of Destiny: No wonder he morphed into a human juggernaut, his first rugby ball was given to him by another player who was simply nails – ex-international centre, Dr Jack Matthews. How could JPR fail to join the Welsh hard men elite after that start in life?

The Full-back Pioneer: Before JPR, tries scored by full-backs were like buses – it took 87 years to get two (one from Vivian Jenkins in 1934 and Keith Jarrett 108 games later in 1967) – and then six came along from a single no. 15. JPR created an entirely new offensive role for the last line of defence, becoming the prototype of the modern full-back in the process.

The Wimbledon Wonder: Most Welsh internationals were raised with jumpers for goal-posts but young Japes was lucky enough to have his own tennis court in the back garden. In 1966 he beat a young David Lloyd 6–4, 6–4 to win a British Junior singles title at Wimbledon. The following year he defeated Dick Stockton and Sandy Meyer en route to the Canadian junior title. But selection for the 1969 Welsh rugby tour to Argentina sealed his choice of sport.

THE STATS Wales: **55** Caps British & Irish Lions: **8** Caps

Lion Rampant: If you're only going to drop one goal in your career make it one that really counts. JPR's 50-yarder in the fourth Test against the All Blacks in 1971 secured the 14–14 draw which clinched the Lions only ever series win in New Zealand. In the 1974 Lions tour of South Africa his fame rested on thundering 60 metres down the pitch to lamp Moaner van Heerden when the '99' call came.

Shouldering a Grand Slam: Only one thing stood between Jean-François Gourdon, the try line and a French Grand Slam in 1976 – JPR's shoulder. He used it to smash the Gallic wing into touch and bring the Grand Slam home to Wales.

Casualty Courage: If there had been a blood bin in the 70s, JPR's career would have been cut by half. But not even a brutal double raking across his face from All Black prop John Ashworth kept him off the field for long. Two lost pints of blood later and 30 stitches from his dad and the Bridgend captain was back. When not sustaining enough injuries to fill his own A&E department, the medical student who became an orthopaedic surgeon was tending other stricken players – as grateful All Black Bob Burgess will testify.

The Old Enemy's Nemesis: JPR ended his international career against England in 1981. Five of his six tries for Wales were scored against the men in white, ensuring the remarkable stat of a 100 per cent victory record in 12 matches.

But did anything faze Wales's most fearless warrior? Yes – women in labour! As a nervous young medic JPR suddenly found himself in the maternity department. 'Every student needed 20 deliveries under his belt, so to speak,' he recalls. 'The first birth that I witnessed was bad enough but my first delivery was a terrifying shock… my ability to cope with the squeamish side of the job was tested to the full!' If he started out catching slippery newborns, no wonder he was always rock-solid under the high ball…

Clubs: London Welsh, Natal, Tondu, Barbarians

FAVOURITE FOREIGNERS
The opponents we loved in the 1970s

When Will Carling was a young boy he was so obsessed with the Welsh team of the 70s, he was disappointed to find out he wasn't actually Welsh himself. Though Welsh fans during that decade obviously never had any allegiance problems, it didn't stop them admiring the talents of players from opposing teams. These were some of our favourite foreigners.

Jean-Pierre Rives – France

France has produced some of the world's greatest philosophers. In the 70s it sent one on to the field in the form of Jean-Pierre Rives. 'The whole point of rugby is that it is, first and foremost, a state of mind, a spirit,' mused the flanker.

Not that he was ever quiet and pensive on the pitch, of course. The blond bombshell of Les Bleus' back row embodied the courage, charisma and commitment of French forward play. Famed for his fearless approach, the Toulouse-born cult hero frequently underlined his warrior status by finishing a game plastered in blood.

Nicknamed 'Casque d'Or' (Blond Helmet) by the French faithful, he won 59 caps – 34 as captain, and was France's Grand Slam skipper in 1977. Alongside Jean-Claude Skrela and Jean-Pierre Bastiat he formed one of the most formidable back-row combinations in the history of the game.

After retiring from rugby in 1984 Rives rekindled his boyhood passion for art and has since carved out a successful career as a sculptor.

70s French cult hero. An uncharacteristically unbloodied Jean-Pierre Rives takes the field against Wales at Parc des Princes in 1977.

David Duckham – England

For an English player called David could there be any greater accolade from the Welsh rugby public than being re-named Dai? The affectionate epithet was awarded after Duckham shone as the only English back in the Barbarians team that beat the All Blacks at Cardiff Arms Park in 1973.

Duckham delighted the Welsh crowd that day with a dazzling break through the New Zealand defence. The winger's twinkle-toed move left commentator Cliff Morgan unsure whether he'd dummied or side-stepped. The cameraman was similarly bamboozled. Duckham's jink sent the lens to the right while he stepped out of shot to the left.

The man from Coventry had already discovered his inner Welshman on the 1971 Lions tour. Here, Carwyn James encouraged Duckham to play with more adventure than he expressed in the England shirt. Given free rein, the powerful, swerving wing scored 11 tries in his 16 games on tour.

When Duckham retired, he acknowledged the compliment Welsh rugby fans paid him with the title of his autobiography – *Dai For England*.

Dai Duckham, Barbarian and honorary Welshman, dummies extravagantly past All Blacks Bob Burgess and Ian Hurst (no. 12) at Cardiff in 1973.

The Big Man, Willie John McBride of Ireland.

Willie John McBride – Ireland

The big man who played on five Lions tours was revered by his Welsh team-mates on those southern hemisphere odysseys. He is the legends' legend.

An Ulsterman of farming stock, Willie John was a natural leader on and off the pitch. Captaining the 74 Lions to a record-breaking series win in South Africa, the lock had to steer his men through chaos on the field and carnage in the team hotel.

He applied the Musketeer tactic of '99' to the former situation – all for one and one for all.

The off-pitch scenario demanded more subtle diplomacy. After the second Test victory of 74, the Lions celebrated late into the night and in spirited fashion. Their hotel lobby was a battlefield of broken furniture.

As Willie John stood in his underpants, sucked on his pipe and surveyed the scene, he was confronted by the furious hotel manager. 'What,' said the Lions captain, 'seems to be the problem?'

The manager threatened to call the cops. With visions of hordes of South African riot police arriving on the scene, not to mention damning headlines about idiot rugby tourists, Willie John quietly diffused the tension.

'Excuse me, but if you are going to get the police,' he said to the manager with a smile, 'do you think there will be many of them?'

And the matter was closed.

Broon frae Troon, Scotland's Gordon Brown on Lions lineout duty against South Africa in 1974. Either side of him are props Fran Cotton (left) and Ian 'Mighty Mouse' McLauchlan.

Gordon Brown – Scotland

While the female fans of Wales may have had a passing fancy for Andy Irvine – who was the nearest thing the Scottish back line got to the boyish charm of a Bay City Roller – the aficionados appreciated lovable lock Gordon Brown.

A giant of a man with a big heart, Broon frae Troon, as he was universally known, was adored throughout the world of rugby. A bedrock of the Lions pack through the 71, 74 and 77 tours, he was considered the perfect second-row all-rounder by Carwyn James.

His courage for the cause on the 71 tour saw him receive 20 stitches in the final Test. And his joie de vivre and storytelling talents off the pitch endeared him to his team-mates.

Brown formed a particular bond with Bobby Windsor, whom he liked to describe as 'the archetypal lovable rogue' while joking about checking he still had his watch and rings after a handshake from the Welsh hooker.

But the strength of their friendship was revealed in the aftermath of Brown's death from cancer in 2001, aged just 53. 'I rang Gordon most weekends for the last eight months of his life,' said Windsor. 'And every time before I rang off, I told him I loved him. And that's something I've never told any other bloke…'

Wheel of misfortune. Second-row stalwart Geoff Wheel is sent off against Ireland at Cardiff in 1977, and is consoled on his way from the field by 1970s team physio Gerry Lewis.

When is a *Grand Slam* not a Grand Slam? (1977)

Phil Bennett took over the captain's armband as Wales started the Five Nations championship for the first time with a match against Ireland in Cardiff. The game brought another championship first... red cards. Welsh lock Geoff Wheel and Irish no. 8 Willie Duggan were both sent off in the 37th minute for punching. A Welsh side featuring three new caps – David Burcher, Jeff Squire and Clive Burgess – didn't cut loose until the final stages, transforming a 10–9 lead into a more convincing 25–9 margin with a late flurry of points.

Wales were cheered to victory from a revamped North Enclosure that was now largely seated, perhaps depriving the standing, swaying beer-monsters of their usual fun but also ensuring

1977 Newport New Boy, David Burcher played a part in the greatest Welsh try of the decade. His support player at Murrayfield here is another new boy, Aberavon prop Clive Williams.

Gareth Edwards's last try against England. The forlorn Englishmen are Mike Slemen (prostrate and obscured) and (from l. to r.) Martin Cooper, Roger Uttley and Mike Rafter. Derek Quinnell is the Welsh no. 8.

to the relief of many that al fresco toilet trips were a thing of the past.

In France the makers of BBC Wales comedy *Grand Slam* were hoping for a Welsh win as they filmed the adventures of Windsor Davies and co. around the real-life action of the match. But Wales departed from the script with a lacklustre performance that saw them slump to a 16–9 defeat at Parc Des Princes. The Grand Slam would eventually go to their Gallic opponents that season.

A Triple Crown was still on the cards after Wales bounced back with a 14–9 win against England, achieved with impressive forward dominance. Now they had to go to Murrayfield… and Gareth Edwards had to get back from

America, where he had squeezed in an appearance in the World Superstars contest in Georgia. He arrived back from the multi-sport competition that was a staple of 70s television just in time to make the Thursday run-out before catching the Edinburgh plane.

The Crown-clinching match included an absolute jewel of a try – arguably the greatest team try of the decade. Under the posts, Phil Bennett finished off a move that began deep in Wales's own half with a jinking Gerald Davies and swept through the skillset of Bennett, Burcher and Fenwick en route. J.J. Williams also scored, Bennett converted both tries and added two penalties to the 18–9 victory that brought Wales its 14th Triple Crown.

Superstar actor Richard Burton, a rugby man through and through. (*BBC*)

13m. LSD tablets found

£100M. DRUGS HAUL IN MID WALES

THE BIGGEST drugs haul ever in Britain has been
remote farmhouse in Mid-Wales. They fou
preaching £100 million.
A number of people have
based in the

WESTERN MAIL

Judge sends drug gang down for 120 years

PURE LSD TABLETS 'MUST
HAVE REACHED
PEOPLE OF ALL AGES'

Also in 1977: Centred on west Wales, Operation Julie broke up one of the largest LSD manufacturing operations in the world, uncovering evidence of exporting to 100 countries and supplying 90% of the UK's LSD. Welsh police officers assumed hippy garb to go undercover. Craig Thomas – son of rugby writing great JBG – published the best selling thriller *Firefox*. Mount Stuart Primary School in Cardiff appointed the first female black head teacher in Wales. Richard Burton received his sixth Best Actor Academy Award nomination for *Equus*… and didn't win the Oscar yet again. The first UK athletics championships were held at Cwmbran and Johnny 'Matchstick Man' Owen won the British bantamweight title. BBC Radio Wales and Radio Cymru were established. Comedian Ryan Davies died at just 40.

GRAND SLAM, THE MOVIE

"It's an absolute classic"
Roy Noble, BBC Radio Wales & S4C

GRAND SLAM

15

Starring Windsor Davies
& Huw Griffiths

Go the whole hog, Mog!

They say what goes on tour stays on tour but in 1977 Grand Slam brought it on to our television screens, *immortalising* the colour and characters of a Welsh rugby weekend in Paris. The television comedy became an instant classic, spawning catchphrases that every rugby fan can still recite.

It was created by the acclaimed playwright Gwenlyn Parry and John Hefin, who would go on to produce some of the great Welsh television dramas, including *The Life and Times of Lloyd George.*

It is the tale of a group of Welsh supporters heading for the stands of Parc des Princes via the fleshpots of Pigalle, where Windsor Davies as Mog Jones reminds his posse, as only an Hon Sec can, that they are 'ambassadors for Wales', in the city where 'you'll see it all, kid'.

Father and son undertakers Glyn (Dewi 'Pws' Morris) and Mr Lloyd Evans (Hugh Griffith) regard each other with a Steptoe and Son-like grudging affection.

'I know your smells,' growls the latter to the former. Utterly convincing as a French femme fatale, Sharon Morgan provides saucy chic... and a boudoir for Glyn to watch the game.

And then there's boutique owner Maldwyn Novello-Pughe (Siôn Probert), he's here, he's there and he's everywhere,

so beware. Maldwyn, possibly the only Welsh male to go on tour in a fun fur, is as imaginative with his one-liners as his window displays – whether he's expressing the joy of retail therapy: 'I'll be down that boulevard like a bat out of hell!' or explaining the mysteries of the hotel bidet: 'It's for your downstairs, not your upstairs!'

Star of *Grand Slam* Dewi 'Pws' Morris (*BBC*)

What better subject could a 1977 comedy embrace, given that that the success of that sensational Welsh team had already seeped into popular culture? Max Boyce provided the laughter soundtrack in song, John Hughes moulded rugby humour in clay Groggs and cartoonist Gren made it picture perfect. Now it was to find hilarious expression on the small screen.

The spur-of-the-moment comedy was complemented by reportage-style camerawork – a cutting edge approach 40 years ago. Scottish cameramen Russ Walker filmed the action as if it were a documentary.

Yet if the filming of *Grand Slam* thrived on this sense of unpredictability, one thing was for certain – Wales would win, providing the film with its perfect denouement.

They had the year before. They would the year after. But in 1977 the Grand Slam eluded Wales. Jean-Pierre Rives may have had his roots showing – as Maldwyn so memorably spotted – but on that Saturday in Parc des Princes he was a blond having far more fun than his opponents. The flaxen-haired flanker was part of a fearsome French pack which squeezed the life out of Wales. They lost 16–9.

'I'm used to his smells': Oscar-winning Welsh actor Hugh Griffith brought his own Hollywood glamour to *Grand Slam*.
(*PA Images*)

SUPER SUPPORTERS
The Adventures of Wiljo and Lyn

Wiljo Salen was a young law student from Brecon as the decade began while Eiluned John, raised in Llanharan, was a teacher and young mother. Indeed the only game she missed in the 70s – England v Wales 1972 – was viewed from the maternity ward after giving birth to her first child Owen. 'I'd wanted to call him Gareth but my cousin had pinched the name for one of her twins so I gave my son Gareth's second name.' She was back for the Scotland match a few weeks later.

Eiluned 'Lyn' John with Jeff Squire:
'I won a Welsh jersey for a competition in the *Western Mail* describing my greatest 70s rugby moment. They thought 'Lyn' was a man! I nearly got left in the foyer of the newspaper office when they just looked over my head and went away. I had to ask if I was going to get my jersey. But I ended up on the back page – hooray!' (*Western Mail*)

Gordon Brown charges at Ray Gravell with Sandy Carmichael on his shoulder. A world-record 104,000 were at Murrayfield to see Scotland beat Wales in 1975. Eiluned John was one of them! (*PA Images*)

Random Recollections

Eiluned: The 70s really started in 1968! One by one the team got together. In 1969 Gareth was captain, the youngest ever versus England. And Wales had a wonderful season. We beat – no trounced – England at home 30–9. Maurice Richards ran riot with four tries and Barry scored a beauty. What a runner he was. He just seemed to glide…

Wiljo: My first away game was Twickers 1970. Gareth off. Chico [Ray Hopkins] on, game won. My tour mate was always Julian Thomas. He was known as Slurper. We stayed with Slurper's sister in London. Her flatmate was Tony Blackburn's secretary. We went to a BBC party in the night, all velvet and corduroy. We didn't last long…

Eiluned: Some games were unticketed. I was there in Murrayfield in 1975 for the biggest crowd ever. I was on the schools bank behind the posts. The turnstiles kept turning with more and more coming in. There was no room to move. Ale was being drunk at one end and coming out nearly the same colour into the same bottle all around us...

Wiljo: We had a brilliant team and crowds that were made up of rugby fans – it wasn't stage-managed. The terraces created a more intense atmosphere. The lack of corporates meant that every one there was there for rugby which increased the intensity. The singing was like a church choir fuelled by alcohol and was fantastic. Memories are obviously coloured by the fact that we always seemed to win…

Eiluned: Not much money, college, marrying, young kids, mortgage, but with a willing widowed Mam to babysit and some planning and saving we went to Paris and Edinburgh every two years. Even in the early days of grotty b&bs we laughed and laughed. We kept winning even when losing players. We didn't mind the odd loss but we *had* to beat England and we usually did.

Players had other jobs, still went to college, worked in pits and steelworks. The money factor hadn't tainted the game. Players progressed from village rugby to the town/city clubs. Clubs brought communities together….

Player Profile
GERALD DAVIES

David Parry-Jones once penned a memorably poetic paragraph on how Gerald Davies electrified the game with the voltage of his sidestepping brilliance. But David Duckham, English opponent and Lions team-mate, had a more prosaic assessment, based on the practical experience of trying to mark him:

'You know he is going to sidestep. You also know there isn't a thing you can do about it.'

A god-fearing gallop: We may have the topography of Carmarthenshire to thank for the fleet feet that defined Gerald's career. Born in Llansaint, the son of a miner would race home from training sessions at Queen Elizabeth Grammar School, and with good reason. Having got off the bus and with a two-and-a-half-mile climb to the village, he had to pass three cemeteries on the way. And as he admits, having been brought up the strict Nonconformist way with all its threats of fire and brimstone, he fairly sprinted past those gravestones.

(Western Mail)

(Getty Images)

From 10 to 12 to 13 to 14: Gerald began his schoolboy international career at outside half and made his debut for Wales – against Australia in 1966 – in the centre, where he would stay for a further 11 caps. But on the Wales tour of New Zealand in 1969 coach Clive Rowlands persuaded him to move to the right wing. 'You don't want to get involved with the heavy mob in midfield,' canny Rowlands told the player who, at 11st 7lbs, was certainly more silky than crash-ball. He might have been on the wing but he became central to Welsh success in the 70s.

THE STATS Wales: **46** Caps British & Irish Lions: **5** Caps

Cambridge exams before All Black Tests: If he was poetry in motion on the pitch, off it he liked to read it. In 1970, as Wales were embarking on their golden decade, he made himself unavailable for the entire international season to concentrate on getting his English degree at Cambridge – where he studied after Loughborough.

Finals over, he joined the triumphant 1971 Lions tour and emerged as one of its brightest talents, scoring three Test tries including a crucial one in the third Test. New Zealanders also still recall the way he befuddled the entire Hawkes Bay backline to score a quartet of stunning tries. He subjected Pontypool to a similar fate in a Schweppes Cup match in 1977 with four sprinting tries from near the halfway line to win the game for Cardiff.

Club and Country: Gerald played quite of bit of his rugby in England, notably with London Welsh in its early 70s pomp, he returned to Cardiff – beating Gareth Edwards to the captaincy in its centenary year.

Gerald captained the Welsh side twice – once in a non-capped game against Tonga and in his final appearances in the red shirt on the 1978 tour of Australia. He ended his 12-year international career as joint Welsh-try record holder – sharing the accolade with his great friend Gareth Edwards.

His first post-retirement move was from jink to ink, writing on the game for *The Times* for three decades. He also turned his talents to rugby administration with the WRU, IRB and the British and Irish Lions.

A rugby style guru: Known as one of the more dapper Welsh players of the 70s, Gerald's personal grooming was in keeping with his playing style – collar up, Sgt Pepper moustache, flowing raven hair. Only his shorts were chosen for comfort over appearance. When his team-mates received the starched black match-day issue pair, he'd swiftly swap them for his greying boil-washed favourites in his kit bag. Off the field, he was the picture of 70s elegance, accessorised with cravat and a John Fowles novel, for that classic 'Gutted I'm not playing tomorrow' eve of match picture favoured by the *Western Mail* (left).

Ray of the Rovers. Scotland's defence are not about to deny Ray Gravell his first try for Wales.

Western Mail
WALES v SCOTLAND
SPECIAL 8-PAGE PREVIEW

CARDIFF ARMS PARK
SATURDAY FEB. 10th 1978

WALES v. SCOTLAND
SPECTACULAR

WALES
J. P. R. WILLIAMS 15
(Bridgend)

| T. G. R. DAVIES 14 | R. GRAVELL 13 | S. FENWICK 12 | J. J. WILLIAMS 11 |
| (Cardiff) | (Llanelli) | (Bridgend) | (Llanelli) |

G. O. EDWARDS 9   P. BENNETT (capt.) 10
(Cardiff)   (Llanelli)

D. L. QUINNELL 8
(Llanelli)

| T. J. COBNER 7 | A. J. MARTIN 4 | G. A. D. WHEEL 5 | J. SQUIRE 6 |
| (Pontypool) | (Aberavon) | (Swansea) | (Newport) |

A. G. FAULKNER 1   R. W. WINDSOR 2   G. PRICE 3
(Pontypool)   (Pontypool)   (Pontypool)

Referee: J. R. WEST (Ireland). Kick-off: 3.0

| J. McLAUCHLAN 1 | C. DEANS 2 | N. E. K. PENDER 3 |
| (Jordanhill) | (Hawick) | (Hawick) |

| C. B. HEGARTY 7 | A. J. TOMES 4 | A. F. McHARG 5 | M. A. BIGGAR 6 |
| (Hawick) | (Hawick) | (L. Scottish) | (L. Scottish) |

D. S. M. MacDONALD 8
(West of Scotland)

D. W. MORGAN (Capt.) 9   I. R. McGEECHAN 10
(Stewart's-Melville FP)   (Headingley)

| D. SHEDDEN 11 | A. G. CRANSTON 12 | J. M. RENWICK 13 | W. B. GAMMELL 14 |
| (West of Scotland) | (Hawick) | (Hawick) | (Edin. Wands.) |

B. H. HAY 15
(Boroughmuir)

SCOTLAND

● Record for most tries scored by an individual in Wales v. Scotland matches is held by Ian Smith, who touched down four times for Scotland in 1925.

Triple Triple Crown and Third Grand Slam (1978)

Gareth Edwards celebrated his 50th cap at a rain-lashed Twickenham. It was a rather dour, tryless affair as Wales edged it by three penalties to England's two but their defence of the championship was off to a winning start. Scotland at home provided more colour – particularly when Ray Gravell's only international try saw him swamped by smiling, congratulatory team-mates. Derek Quinnell scored a corker too, thundering up the touchline and palming off three defenders in his powerful wake. It was a move his son Scott would replicate almost exactly in 1994. And Gareth Edwards contributed his 20th and final try for Wales in fine style with a jink, a hand-off and a burst through a tackle.

A few hours after the final whistle the worst blizzard for 30 years hit South Wales confining the Welsh team to the Angel Hotel until the following Monday. Scotland just managed to escape home via Birmingham airport but many of their fans remained stranded for up to a week. Not that they seemed to mind.

Wales arrived in Dublin contemplating a feat that had never been achieved in the Five Nations before – the Triple Triple Crown. It took a monumental effort to secure this prize for the third successive season. Wales built a 13–3 lead but Ireland clawed their way back to 13–all in a match full of fire and fury. Both were directed at JPR for his late tackle on Irish captain Mike Gibson, who was marking his then world record

Snow sad... Visibly heartbroken Scottish supporters stranded in Cardiff.
(Western Mail)

Slam Lake: (l. to r.) Jeff Squire, Derek Quinnell and Allan Martin strike balletic poses as they win this lineout against France's Francis Haget (no. 4).

Western Mail
WALES v FRANCE
12 PAGE GRAND SLAM SPECIAL · CARDIFF ARMS PARK · SATURDAY MARCH 10 1978

The greatest Grand Slam?

By J. B. G. THOMAS

IT SEEMS a bit silly when you look at it this way, on the morning of Grand Slam 1978 between Wales and France at Cardiff Arms Park, but more British people drink French wine than ever before, and more Frenchmen—and women—watch rugby.

Why? The French gave our rather cold isles a liking for good wine, and who can refuse a claret with body or a gently perfumed sauterne? In return we sent across the Channel our rugby men to proselytise for a new religion: RUGBY.

The triple Triple Crown champions

Mules turned into thoroughbreds

A long, long while ago French rugby players, like French lovers, were visionaries, individualists and romantics. Put any eight of them together and expect any marked degree of uniformity was like expecting Welsh forwards not to go over the top in rucks. But an amazing man called Lucien Mias changed all that.

64th cap. The Welsh full-back was booed every time he touched the ball.

The game turned for Wales with a fine try for J.J. Williams, who gathered Fenwick's lobbed pass to win the sprint for the line. Fenwick had also contributed a try himself in the first half while his kicking brought his personal match tally to 16 points in Wales's 20–16 victory.

For Gerald Davies, this was one of the defining matches of the decade: 'When we talk about the strength, the will, the stubbornness of that Welsh team during that period, of not letting go because it meant too much to us and our reputation, the Triple Triple Crown game embodies that.

'We had won the game at one stage but we had to win it a second time and we had to drag ourselves up by our bootstraps to do it. I will never forget how silent the dressing room was after the game was over because we had given our all to win.'

France arrived in Cardiff for a momentous decider, with both sides chasing the Grand Slam. It would also be a game that signalled a closing chapter as both Gareth Edwards and Phil Bennett decided it would be their last game for Wales. They shone to the very end. Bennett produced what many regard to be his best performance in the red jersey, scoring two crucial tries while Edwards dropped a vital long-range goal.

As their 16–7 win delivered the third Grand Slam of the 70s to a nation that had come to expect nothing less, John Dawes commented: 'This team deserves to be recognised as one of the greatest of all time.'

For the players who had formed the core of the side through the decade there was a certain symmetry to their achievement, framed by the 71 and 78 Grand Slams. While the first Grand Slam was a breakthrough for an exuberant young side bursting with talent yet unused to winning, the third was testament to the hard-headed resilience of a team who could not bear to lose.

'The record books will show it was a decade of success if not year on year, certainly for long periods of time, but the game changed,' said Gerald Davies. 'In 78 the Grand Slam was still exciting but it was more constructive. In 71 it was more like one move and chase it!

'The French game was always the important game. It was always us against them. It defined each season, it defined the period. Wales and France were always competing for the big prizes every time. So in 71 when we first did it in Paris it was a major success in my view because it was an indication of where we might go in the future...

'So you take 71 as the beginning of the confidence and then you take 78 where what had been achieved in the meantime meant so much that we couldn't let go. That gave it a theme for the whole period.'

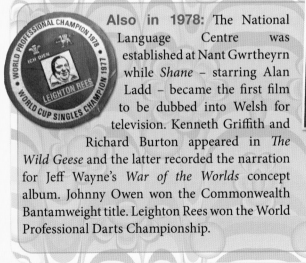

Also in 1978: The National Language Centre was established at Nant Gwrtheyrn while *Shane* – starring Alan Ladd – became the first film to be dubbed into Welsh for television. Kenneth Griffith and Richard Burton appeared in *The Wild Geese* and the latter recorded the narration for Jeff Wayne's *War of the Worlds* concept album. Johnny Owen won the Commonwealth Bantamweight title. Leighton Rees won the World Professional Darts Championship.

Johnny Owen of Merthyr, the bravest of all bantamweights. (*BBC*)

GARETH EDWARDS

He's been voted the Greatest Player of All Time; he scored the Greatest Try of All Time and there's even a statue of him in the Welsh capital. Sir Gareth Edwards is the icons' icon. For rugby lovers across the world he's the player who simply *is* Welsh rugby. Yet when this scrum-half scorched his meteoric path through the 70s, embodying the golden generation, he modestly reckoned: 'We didn't feel we were so special at the time.'

Mentored to greatness: Gareth was taught by a PE master who recognised his potential from the moment the 12-year-old reported to his gymnasium in Pontardawe Technical College in 1959.

Gareth's visionary teacher Bill Samuel nurtured his prize pupil all the way to a scholarship place at Britain's most prestigious sporting school – Millfield. Gareth could have excelled at anything – soccer, gymnastics, athletics – but it was Bill who threw him the rugby ball. 'I didn't choose rugby, rugby chose me.' Football also chose him – he was offered a professional contract by Swansea… but his rugby-loving Mam, Annie-Mary, hid the letter behind the mantelpiece clock.

Dreams of Wales on Archie's Field: As a boy growing up in Gwaun-cae-Gurwen, collier's son Gareth followed the older lads to Cae Archie, the patch of grass where he and his pals enacted their first defeats of England. At night his bedtime prayers had a sporting theme: 'Please God, if I could play just once for Wales, that would be enough.' After some average school reports he returned home to find a miner's helmet and some hobnail boots on the table.

'I see you've got new boots, Dad,' said Gareth.

'Oh no no,' his father replied. 'Try them on. They're for you.'

'Why's that Dad?'

'Well you're not working in school are you? I just want to fit you up. This will be your job.'

That night Gareth's prayers took a little longer: 'I must work harder. I don't want to wear those boots!'

THE STATS Wales: **53** Caps British & Irish Lions: **10** Caps

First cap... and the captaincy by 20: Gareth played his first game for Wales against France aged 19. 'I picked up the jersey, held it lovingly in my hands and kissed the badge. I probably did that before every match I played for Wales.' A mere year later he would be captaining his country. At 20 years and seven months, this made him the world's youngest Test skipper. But it proved a somewhat premature appointment. He was replaced in the role by John Dawes in 1970, allowing the young scrum-half to focus fully on his phenomenal game.

Try, try and tries again: In the years that followed, whether paired with Barry John or Phil Bennett, Gareth created the moments that are seared into the collective memory of 70s rugby. There are the two tries that regularly top the greatest ever polls – the Baa Baas score and the dive into the Arms Park mud that Spike Milligan deemed divine. 'Edwards was a poet that day, not a rugby player,' wrote the awestruck comedian. 'He was a ballet dancer, a pugilist, a mathematician. He was a miracle.'

(Getty Images)

Edwards the Showman: The great entertainer's charisma was not confined to the pitch. When asked by the Welsh selectors to prove his fitness after a hamstring injury he promptly performed a back somersault in the foyer of the Angel Hotel.

He donned a boater and blazer to croon alongside Welsh comic duo Ryan and Ronnie in a television special and remains the only Welsh rugby player to make the charts (the Welsh language ones). In 1972 he teamed up with folk singer Maralene Powell to record a cover version of the 60s hit 'Did You Ever?' ('Wyt Ti Weithiau').

Space odyssey for a 50th cap: By the time he retired after 53 consecutive caps, Gareth held the Welsh record for most appearances and most tries – the latter shared jointly with Gerald Davies. In 1977 he had become the first Welsh player to reach the milestone of 50 caps. To mark the occasion, the WRU presented him with a second cap. In 1998, that iconic piece of velvet was sent into space. When Dr Dafydd Rhys Williams became the first Welsh astronaut, he wanted to take a piece of Welsh memorabilia with him on the Columbia shuttle.

The WRU obliged and the cap took a 6.3 million mile odyssey around the planet in 263 orbits before being returned to its proud owner – the player who was also out of this world.

Clubs: Cardiff, Barbarians

Charlie Faulkner seems happy to carry the ball and Ireland's Mike Gibson over the line.

TOP TEN TRIES

10 Ray 'Chico' Hopkins – England v Wales 1970

Wales were trailing England 13–6 at Twickenham when Gareth Edwards limped off injured. His replacement, Ray Hopkins, made an immediate impact, creating a try for JPR with a blindside burst from a Welsh scrum. Then came his own try – a score that ensured Wales won the match. As England threw to the tail of their lineout and the ball arrived helpfully on the Welsh side, the diminutive man from Maesteg scooped it up and dived through to score in a single movement. Wales hadn't lost at Twickenham for 17 years – in his precious 20 minutes on the field Chico ensured their record remained intact.

9 Charlie Faulkner – Wales v Ireland 1975

Mervyn Davies peeled off the back of an untidy Welsh scrum to get the ball to Phil Bennett. The fly-half sent J.J. Williams on the burst but as the winger passed to Bobby Windsor it was the hooker's speed that astonished the crowd. The Duke positively galloped up field through the Irish defence, managing to give the scoring pass to his brother in arms Charlie Faulkner before he was finally felled. The grin on JJ's face as he greeted the try-scoring prop with arms aloft said it all.

8 Barry John – France v Wales 1971

No-one could glide and sway and ghost-like Barry John – as Max Boyce said: 'He could run through a field of corn and only the corn would know which way he went.' The French defenders certainly couldn't track his path as he weaved his way through them to the whitewash after stepping his opposite number Jean-Louis Berot. Only centre Roland Bertranne came within reach. But at the last moment, Barry changed course once more, befuddled Bertanne and swept over for the Grand Slam winning try.

7 J.P.R. Williams – England v Wales 1976

JPR was always a warrior but the Old Enemy in particular propelled him into frontline battle-mode. He was never on a losing side against England and in three successive visits to Twickenham he scored four tries. Two of them came in 1976 in the victory the press dubbed 'JPR's match'.

The first of those two tries is his entry in this Top 10. The strength of his finish sealed a stylish team move. It began when Mervyn Davies got the ball away from a scrum despite an almighty shove from the English pack. It swept through the backs from Gareth Edwards, to Steve Fenwick to Phil Bennett to J.J. Williams but just as the winger looked as if he might be clattered into touch he delivered an in-pass to JPR who thundered through two white shirts to crash across the try line.

A warrior's salute. JPR celebrates another try against England.

The game that clinched Wales's second Grand Slam of the 70s was won by five penalty goals and a single try, created by a move that spanned the touchlines in France's 25. As Les Bleus tackled tenaciously, Allan Martin snaffled the ball out of a ruck, fed it to Gareth Edwards who shipped it to Ray Gravell. Grav crashed into contact, slipping a deft pass to Phil Bennett. The fly-half lobbed a long pass to Steve Fenwick who could spy an accelerating J.J. Williams to his left. The winger received the ball and scorched in at the corner.

From deep in his own 25, JPR set off on a rather lonely sprint. At this point only Denzil Williams was attempting to keep up with him but as he was a prop this was a pursuit that could only peter out.

The sound of Welsh fans hollering 'Go on John!' almost drowned out the television commentary yet as two French defenders closed in on JPR it looked as if his dash was doomed. But then he heard a voice much closer to the action shouting: 'Japes! Here!' It was Gareth Edwards, who had tracked the doctor, travelling

past the flagging Denzil to offer assistance. JPR jinked infield, checking the two defenders before throwing a big pass out to the scrum-half who had arrived at full speed like the proverbial cavalry to score in the corner.

 Gerald Davies – Scotland v Wales 1971

With Wales trailing in the dying minutes, a final lineout on the Scottish 25 offered a lifeline as Delme Thomas palmed down the ball on a Scottish throw. The ball swept through the Welsh backline with fluent beauty. Edwards to Barry

Scorching in at the corner, JJ scores against France. (*PA Images*)

John; John Dawes; J.P.R. Williams and out to Gerald Davies on the right wing. In full flow, he curved across the line but as the Scottish defence closed in he couldn't quite get near enough to the posts to deliver a simple conversion.

And with the score at 18–17 only that conversion could seal the match. The task of this death or glory kick almost on the touchline was given to left-footed flanker John Taylor, who promptly delivered 'the greatest conversion since St Paul'.

 Graham Price – France v Wales 1975

Geoff Wheel hacked loose ball on over the halfway line, and Graham gave chase, got there first, and gave it another big boot. With remarkable stamina for a player who had toiled at the scrummaging coalface all afternoon, he pursued it through the broken French defence. The opposition full-back Michel Taffary was closing in but J.J. Williams almost slide-tackled him soccer-style to nudge the ball on a few more yards. It popped up into the prop's hands. Without a defender in sight he carried it over the line and thumped it to the ground.

'They'll never believe it in Pontypool!' declared Nigel Starmer-Smith from the commentary box. But Graham's coach mischievously brought him back down to earth: 'The poker-faced reaction of John Dawes was to ask why I hadn't gone round the posts!'

 Gareth Edwards – Wales v Scotland 1972

Spike Milligan said 'they should build a bloody cathedral to mark the spot'. This is why…

Spotting a gap left by Scottish flanker Roger Arneil, Gareth set off from the halfway line. Ten metres into his sprint, he began to look around for his Shadow. But the usually omnipresent Dai Morris was nowhere to be seen. And neither were any other of his team-mates. Another 30 metres of solo acceleration and only Scottish full-back Arthur Brown was in his eye-line. As the defender moved in, Gareth waited until the last possible moment before chipping the ball over his head. Drawing on his schoolboy high-hurdling champion skills, he didn't even break speed as he followed up with a grubber kick.

With 70 metres of the pitch eaten up, the crowd roared him towards the try line as the cover defence closed in and the ball raced perilously towards the dead-ball line. For those watching the incredible move unfold on television, Bill McLaren echoed the thoughts of every viewer. 'Can he score? It will be a miracle if he could. He may well get there. And he has!'

And he did with a sliding dive to ground the ball. As Gareth emerged with an alarmingly red face, everyone from his mother to Welsh physio Gerry Lewis panicked that this wonderful try had come at a cost. But the 'blood' was nothing more than the scarlet mud of the old greyhound track circuiting the Arms Park. The image of Gareth walking back to position with this instant face-pack provided one of the most iconic images of the 70s.

It would be a miracle if Gareth scored this particular try, said Bill McLaren. He did. And it was.
(*Getty Images*)

1 Phil Bennett – Wales v Scotland 1977

If Gareth Edwards's try against Scotland in 1972 was the ultimate individual score of the decade, Phil Bennett's try against the same opposition five years later crowned the ultimate team effort. Each component of the move encapsulated the skills of those who combined to create it.

It began deep in Scotland's half. 'Gerald Davies – what was he doing there?' wondered Bill McLaren. Quite a lot it turned out, as the wing proved the catalyst, sidestepping two Scots, palming off a third, and getting the ball out to Phil Bennett as he finally succumbed to the tackle of the fourth. Bennett burst up to the halfway line, passing to centre David Burcher haring up on his right.

As two navy shirts closed in on him, Burcher delivered the ball basketball-style over their heads to Steve Fenwick. It looked like a hospital pass but Bridgend's blond bombshell flicked the ball out of trouble to Bennett, who jinked past what was left of Scotland's shell-shocked defence to score under the posts, sliding round to face the field with the ball under his chin.

'Oh this is going to be the try of the championship!' purred Bill McLaren. And it's arguably the try of the 70s too.

On his way to the try of the championship and the decade, Phil Bennett beats Ian McLauchlan and Bill Gammell (no. 14).

The elegant Gareth Davies clears his lines watched by the bearded Derek Quinnell and the black-eyed John Richardson of Aberavon.

Winning and Losing (1979)

Despite the transitional nature of the 1979 squad – with the elegant Gareth Davies and flinty Terry Holmes at half back and Elgan Rees, already a capped Lion, arriving on the right wing – the final year of the 70s sustained Welsh success. Defeat by a single point to France denied another Grand Slam but a five-try flourish against England in the final game ensured the championship and a fourth consecutive Triple Crown belonged to Wales.

Yet there were signs that an era was drawing to a close throughout that Five Nations. The Pontypool Front Row packed down for the final time in Paris while at the end of the England match J.J. Williams decided to hang up the boots that had chipped and chased to glory so many times. And John Dawes also bade farewell. Never had the old adage 'quit while you're ahead' seemed more apposite. Spanning the 70s as a player and a coach, Dawes could reflect on the previous 11 seasons in which Wales had won nine championships, six Triple Crowns and three Grand Slams.

Between 1969 and 1979, of the 43 games played in the Five Nations, Wales won 33, lost seven and drew three. This remarkable record included 10 victories over England. When the Old Enemy won the Grand Slam in 1980 – their first outright win of the championship since 1963 – Welsh fans had to concede the glory days were over in the most painful way possible. And they faced a long wait to see the dragon roar once more.

Neath, Wales and Lions wing, 'Intercity' Elgan Rees, with Graham Price.

The flinty Terry Holmes gets his pass away from New Zealand's Dave Loveridge during the controversial 1978 international.

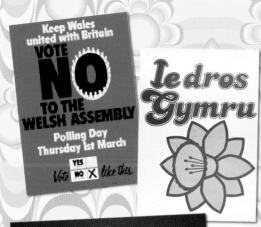

Also in 1979: In the referendum on St David's Day Wales voted 'No' to Devolution. In the Rhondda, formidable councillor Annie Powell became Britain's first Communist mayor, while Labour's Ann Clwyd was among the newly-elected MEPs in the Euro elections. Katharine Hepburn starred in a film version of the Welsh classic *The Corn is Green*. In his first year as a professional, Terry Griffiths won snooker's World Championship.

Another Llanelli-born sporting star, Terry Griffiths (right) with Dennis Taylor, whom he defeated to become world snooker champion in 1979.
(*PA Images*)

MEDIA MAIN MEN

Not only did Welsh rugby's fortunes change dramatically during the 1970s, the way the game was broadcast and reported changed. The rugby media was as much a part of our experience as the game which they portrayed.

In 1970 BBC Wales made its first television programme in colour – lavishing its new rainbow spectrum on its coverage of the Llangollen Eisteddfod. But as the decade progressed, it would be Welsh rugby that really benefited from this technological leap forward as red shirts ran riot across the green green grass of home.

The game discovered colour in more ways than one – literally on the television screen and metaphorically in the commentary of such wonder wordsmiths as Bill McLaren. But who else was who?

John Brinley George Thomas

Universally known as JBG, this cigar-toting doyen of rugby writing influenced the game as much as he reflected it.

The son of a Pontypridd butcher, who joined the *Western Mail* in 1946 as chief rugby writer and left it 36 years later as assistant editor, he was revered by fans and players alike. And in JBG, The Big Five – the legendary Welsh team selection panel – had a secret sixth member.

As sports journalist Rob Cole pointed out: 'The effect his writing was able to generate is best illustrated by the fact that his editor once told him to "make a few mistakes" when predicting the Welsh team so that the readers of the *Western Mail* would not think it was he who picked the national side.'

Alun Williams (*BBC*)

Alun Williams

Combining energy and eloquence with a waspish wit, Williams' vivid commentary on the all-conquering 74 Lions transported listeners to the stands of South Africa via their transistors:

'JJ Williams the kick ahead. Over the 25. He's racing for it. He's beaten everybody. Can he get over? Yes! JJ Williams has scored again! (Adopts strong Valleys accent) What a player!'

Cliff Morgan

One of the greatest of all Welsh outside halves showed exactly how words should be matched to television pictures. His musicality probably helped. As a player he was the team choir-master, as a commentator his speech rhythms were always on the beat of the images in front of him. Morgan's description of Gareth Edwards' iconic Barbarians try against the All Blacks is often quoted as the greatest rugby commentary ever.

Cliff Morgan, legendary fly-half and broadcaster, in the company of Tom Jones and David Frost. (*PA Images*)

Bill McLaren

The Voice of Rugby, McLaren's folksy metaphors were underpinned by forensic research, his crib-sheets listed every possible stat next to players' names in spidery shorthand. This meticulous attention to detail ensured McLaren was, quite literally, never lost for words.

And he coined some magical phrases on the Welsh greats of the 70s. On Phil Bennett he quipped: 'They say down at Stradey that if you ever catch him you get to make a wish' while his verdict on Gerald Davies was: 'His sidestep was marvellous – like a shaft of lightning.'

Picking up the microphone for the final time to guide viewers through Wales v Scotland in 2002, McLaren paid fulsome tribute to the players who had inspired his most cherished commentaries. 'I will never forget the delight of commentating on the great moments of the 70s when Wales played total rugby.'

Bill McLaren (*BBC*)

David Parry-Jones brought the erudition of an Oxford graduate to rugby reportage and the insight of a man who had been steeped in the game since his youth – from the schoolboy enclosure of the Arms Park in the 1940s to skippering Cardiff Harlequins RFC.

In his trademark sheepskin coat, he cut an elegant and eloquent figure on the Welsh and British rugby scene. And he was as impressive with the written as the spoken word. The award-winning author of 16 sports books – including *The Dawes Decades* – David was also a rugby correspondent and columnist for *The Times* and *Sunday Mirror*.

Dewi Griffiths

Let's not forget those who worked behind the cameras, such as the Rhondda-born producer/director who masterminded the outside broadcasts of internationals. Dewi – who would later become a national treasure through presenting the nostalgic music show *String of Pearls* – also produced *The Crowning Years*. This video became a staple of every rugby fan's collection, not to mention a visual comfort blanket to cling to through the bleaker years of the 1980s.

Dewi Griffiths (second left) (*BBC*)

So the growth of broadcast and print journalism through the 70s helped create the iconography of the era. The players obviously provided the glorious source material but thanks to poetic soundtracks, evocative headlines, colour coverage and powerful images such as the mud-splattered profile of Gareth Edwards the media ensured their deeds were recorded and celebrated as never before.

Joker in the pack
GREN

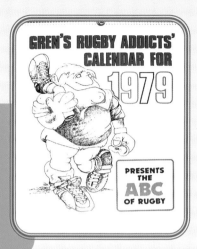

GREN'S RUGBY ADDICTS' CALENDAR FOR 1979

PRESENTS THE **ABC** OF RUGBY

The legendary cartoonist Gren always joked his ambition was to become 'official war artist for the Welsh Rugby Union'. There is certainly no better illustrated history of the game in the 70s than his pen and ink masterpieces.

Born Grenville Jones in Hengoed in 1934, he started drawing comic pictures at the age of eight, selling his first freelance cartoon to the *Birmingham Mail* in the early 1960s.

After five years as an engineering designer and a precarious spell as a freelance, selling cartoons to *Whizzer and Chips*, his breakthrough came with a staff cartoonist's job on the *Western Mail* and *South Wales Echo* in 1968 – where he delighted readers with his daily drawings until his death in 2007.

Arriving in time for the dawn of rugby's golden era, Gren reflected and celebrated the character of the game – which he loved dearly – for the rest of his illustrious career.

Aberflyarff

He didn't just mirror the real players in his artwork, he created a fictional rugby universe that every fan could relate to – the village of Aberflyarff in Scrumcap Valley on the River Efflew.

His' Ponty an' Pop' strips brought us players as memorable – though not quite as talented – as their real-life counterparts. Who can forget the likes of Arnold Nutstrampler and Attila Groinstomper? Not to mention the formidable clubhouse barmaid Bromide Lil.

Sheepskin commentaries

Gren's trademark sheep Nigel and Neville also served as a rugby commentary service – their woolly coats bearing incisive views on everything from Welsh selection to match results. He created these ovine icons after driving some visitors through the village of Pontlottyn. As a sheep nonchalantly crossed the road in front of him, he slowed down to let it pass – much to his visitors' surprise.

'They were amazed that I should be treating a sheep like one of the community, which of course, they are in the valleys,' he explained. 'Out of that grew the idea to have Neville and Nigel as characters in the cartoons.'

Boyce's Choice

Gren enjoyed a fruitful creative partnership with Max Boyce, bringing the latter's lyrics and poetry alive in drawings of wondrous detail. His illustrations for Max's 1975 chart-topping album *We All Had Doctors' Papers* earned him a gold disc from EMI – making him the only cartoonist to ever receive this honour.

When Gren died aged 72, the WRU paid tribute to its beloved 'unofficial war artist'. 'Welsh rugby has lost a great friend,' they said. And as Gareth Edwards put it: 'He defined our character and never failed to raise a smile.'

Two of Stradey's finest, Phil Bennett and Ray Gravell, take the field against France in the 1978 Grand Slam decider. Behind them are JPR (left) and Geoff Wheel.

Legend, Folklore and Fun

Rather than end this unashamedly nostalgic trawl through the greatest decade in Welsh rugby history with a heavy heart, better to listen to some of the stories and quotes spawned by this glorious decade, showcasing those players who became national heroes on a scale previously unimagined. This is the stuff of folklore, proof positive of the way rugby in 1970s Wales was so much more than eighty minutes of excitement on a Saturday afternoon.

How the Duke turned into the Pink Punk

Bobby Windsor developed an impressive Mallen Streak in the late 70s but wasn't keen on becoming a silver fox so attempted to disguise it. His secret dyeing sessions were found out when he brought the wrong shade of hair colour on tour and his fringe turned an alarming shade of pink. Years later Graham Price resurrected the tale of the Duke's magenta mane at a reunion dinner. Bobby had recently expressed his horror at the luxuriant

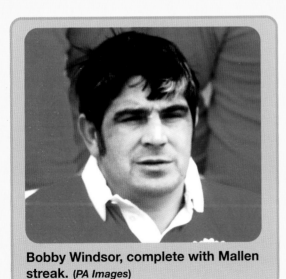

Bobby Windsor, complete with Mallen streak. *(PA Images)*

curls sported by the Welsh Hair Bear props Adam and Duncan Jones.

'At this point I'd just like to remind Bobby of the comments he made about the current Welsh front row,' said Graham. 'You said, "When you run out as a forward, you run out mean and lean as if you are going to do damage. They shouldn't worry about their hair. I would leave that to the girls behind the scrum". And as the room erupted, like the best stand-ups, Bobby got the perfectly-timed last word: 'I was the first punk in Welsh rugby!'

Mrs Mainwaring – the ultimate Rugby Mam

The power of the Welsh Rugby Mam should not be underestimated. In the noughties, it left coach Steve Hansen mystified. He was used to wives and girlfriends grumbling about their other halves incarcerated in training camps but when the Jail of Glamorgan closed its doors, there was a new familial force to contend with: 'It's the mothers you've got to watch in Wales,' he said, 'those Mams don't like being too far away from their boys.'

But perhaps he didn't realise the fine tradition of maternal devotion in Wales that began with the mother of all Rugby Mams, the legendary Evelyn Mainwaring whose fame in the 1970s rivalled that of the players themselves. She was even given an award for services to rugby support by Castella Cigars.

Mrs Mainwaring, who died aged 88 in 2004, set the standard for rugby mother love. Steeped in the game, with five brothers who played for Aberavon, she supported the team for 75 years. But when 'her boy Billy' took the field, she gave the phrase vocal encouragement a whole new meaning.

The legendary Mrs Mainwaring.
(*Western Mail*)

Capped six times for Wales, the Wizards' lock was arguably the most well-supported player in the history of world rugby. His every performance was accompanied by an individual running commentary from the lady in the stands. It had a single theme: 'Get yer hands off my Billy!'

What goes on tour... when Bobby slept with Tommy

On the 1974 tour of South Africa, The Welsh Lions were integral to the fun off the field as well as the fabulous feats on it. In fact, 40 years before Ant and Dec went near a jungle Tommy David and Bobby Windsor were enduring their own episode of *I'm A Celebrity Get Me Out of Here...* in the dead of night in on safari in Kruger Park.

After one of their Sunday night drinking sessions the players were warned of the perils of the snakes, scorpions, spiders they might encounter on their stroll back to their respective huts. It proved too much for Bobby who ended up banging on the door of Tommy David's accommodation in a blind panic. The story is recounted in Clem Thomas's official history of the British Lions.

'He was frightened to death and it takes a lot to frighten anybody who's been shouted at by Ray Prosser,' Tommy explained. ' "Tom" whimpered Bobby – and until you've heard a member of the Pontypool Front Row whimpering, you ain't heard nothing. "Tom, I'm lost. I can't find my 'ut.

Can I sleep with you?" So he climbed into my bed. There was more than 30 stone in that single bed but it didn't seem to worry Bobby. I suppose that anybody who has spent a lot of his time jammed between Graham Price and Charlie Faulkner is used to living rough.'

The pair lay listening to the ominous sounds of the South African night. Bobby reckoned he could hear lions. 'By this time I was holding hands with Bobby, so you can tell what a terrible state he was in. Then it happened and something came hurtling through our mesh window.'

Utter bedlam erupted as the hooker and the flanker shrieked with fear and fought each other to find safety under the bed. The banging increased. And finally the source of the terror was revealed to be lions… but of the British and Irish variety as the hysterical trio of Chris Ralston, Mike Burton and Ian 'Mighty Mouse' McLauchlan burst in to retrieve the log they'd thrown through the window.

'Just the usual sort of prank,' laughed Tommy, 'but enough for me to consider asking Dr Christian Barnard to put me on his waiting list.'

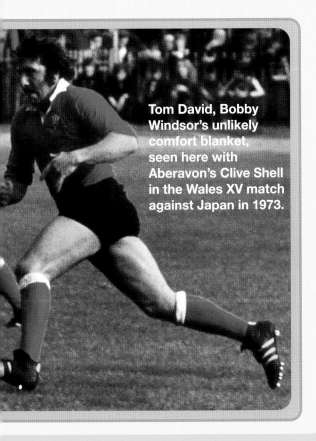

Tom David, Bobby Windsor's unlikely comfort blanket, seen here with Aberavon's Clive Shell in the Wales XV match against Japan in 1973.

'QUOTES'

'Carwyn James was a magical little man. He had this great feeling for rugby football in that he saw it as a piece of opera that should be played with grace and skill.'
— **Willie John McBride** on his Lions coach.

'Gareth Edwards: the sooner that little so-and-so goes to rugby league, the better it will be for us'.
— former English scrum-half **Dickie Jeeps**.

'You've got to get your first tackle in early, even if it's late.'
— **Ray Gravell**

'I prefer rugby to soccer. I enjoy the violence in rugby, except when they start biting each other's ears off.'
— **Elizabeth Taylor**, who Richard Burton took to see Aberavon RFC play.

'I didn't actually see the conversion at the time because I'd retired to the bar to buy my sister Edna a glass of celebratory champagne, so confident was I in JT's ability'
— **Clive Rowlands**'s favourite fib when asked if he watched John Taylor take his famous conversion to beat Scotland in 1971. Though not popping the cork prematurely, he did actually turn his back.

Clive Rowlands

'The main difference between playing League and Union is that now I get my hangovers on a Monday instead of Sunday'
— **Tommy David**

'Bloody typical isn't it? The car's a write-off. The tanker's a write-off. But JPR comes out of it all in one piece.'
— **Gareth Edwards** reflecting on the full-back's indestructibility after his 1978 crash.

J. P. R. Williams

'Ray Gravell Eats Soft Centres'
— Banner at Cardiff Arms Park, 1970s.

'I know… because I Was There.'
— **Max Boyce**

ACKNOWLEDGEMENTS

This book wasn't actually my idea so a huge thank you to Ceri Wyn Jones of Gomer for coming up with such a cracking concept in the first place and steering me through the process with charm, patience and skill.

Not only has writing it allowed me to wallow in the unashamed rugby nostalgia of my childhood – it has enabled me to channel the spirit of all those annuals that were essential reading for those of us who grew up in the 1970s.

Indeed, before I wrote a single word on the deeds of the Golden Era Gods, I enjoyed an internet shopping spree ordering ancient copies of *Jackie* and *Roy of the Rovers* to get into the 70s groove. (I didn't need to buy any *Blue Peter* annuals as I still had 10 of them in pristine condition.)

The words I did eventually write would have had little impact without the fabulously retro page design so thank you to Gary Evans for such authentic 70s artistry. Thank you too Elin Sian Blake for your wonderful portrait of Gareth In The Mud.

Over the years it has been an honour to interview the great players of the 70s who have always indulged my requests for quotes and anecdotes with kindness and patience. I have drawn on the many conversations we have shared for this book so thank you to our Welsh sporting legends for the privilege of your company and insights.

Thanks to Max Boyce who I have worked with in television and radio for 15 years and whose unique perspective on the 70s has always been an inspiration. I was also extremely fortunate to count Groggs creator John Hughes, *Grand Slam* director John Hefin and cartoonist Gren as personal friends. All three, who are sadly no longer with us, were amazing creatives, true gentlemen and contributed so much to the culture that grew around Welsh rugby in that decade. I loved hearing their stories and reflecting on their talents.

I am also grateful to Wiljo Salen and Lyn John, the two fans whose colourful memories of following Wales through that momentous era could have filled a separate book.

Thank you to my family for their support. My wonderful late mother June, who first plonked me in front of the telly for the Five Nations when I was a toddler, would have loved the fact her passion for the game is continuing down the female line. Thank you Dad for doubling as my grammar police and cuttings librarian for 25 years. And thanks too to my older brothers Michael and Adrian, who in 1978 occasionally let me look at their limited edition Wales Grand Slam poster – an experience which might just have set a nine-year-old girl off on a lifelong rugby journey.

Carolyn Hitt

Barbarians 1973

Standing (l. to r.): touch judge, Geoffrey Windsor Lewis (Barbarians secretary), John Pullin, Willie John McBride, Bob Wilkinson; Derek Quinnell, Sandy Carmichael, David Duckham, Georges Domercq (referee), touch judge. Sitting: Gareth Edwards, Mike Gibson, Brigadier Glyn Hughes (Barbarians), John Dawes (captain), Herbert Waddell (Barbarians), John Bevan, Ray McLoughlin. On Ground: Fergus Slattery, Tommy David, Phil Bennett, J.P.R. Williams.

Lions 1971

Back row (l. to r.): Dr Doug Smith, Mike Gibson, Chris Rea, Ian McLauchlan, Fergus Slattery, Sandy Carmichael,
Derek Quinnell, Mike Roberts, John Spencer, Sean Lynch, Delme Thomas, Mike Hipwell, Peter Dixon, Carwyn James.
Middle Row: Ray 'Chico' Hopkins, Willie John McBride, Mervyn Davies,
Gordon Brown, John Dawes, Bob Hiller, John Bevan, Alistair Biggar, John Taylor.
Front Row: Ray McLoughlin, Arthur Lewis, John Pullin, Gareth Edwards, Barry John, Frank Laidlaw, Gerald Davies, J.P.R. Williams, David Duckham.